Frazzled to Free

D0067527

frazzled
to
free

THE SOULFUL MOMMA'S GUIDE TO FINDING MEANINGFUL WORK

KAYLA BERG

NEW YORK

NASHVILLE • MELBOURNE • VANCOUVER

Frazzled to Free

The Soulful Momma's Guide to Finding Meaningful Work

Published in New York, New York, by Morgan James Publishing in partnership with Difference Press. Morgan James is a trademark of Morgan James, LLC. www.MorganJamesPublishing.com

The Morgan James Speakers Group can bring authors to your live event. For more information or to book an event visit The Morgan James Speakers Group at www.TheMorganJamesSpeakersGroup.com.

ISBN 9781683504924 paperback
ISBN 9781683504931 eBook
Library of Congress Control Number: 2017935794

Cover Design by:
Jennifer Stimson

Interior Design by:
Chris Treccani
www.3dogdesign.net

In an effort to support local communities, raise awareness and funds, Morgan James Publishing donates a percentage of all book sales for the life of each book to Habitat for Humanity Peninsula and Greater Williamsburg.

Get involved today! Visit
www.MorganJamesBuilds.com

DEDICATION

For Christopher.

This book would not exist without your love,
support, and mad parenting skills.

TABLE OF CONTENTS

INTRODUCTION

"Everyone has been made for some particular
work, and the desire for that work has been
put in every heart."
–Rumi

We've felt it. That dread of going back to work at an unsatisfying, unfulfilling job and leaving the kids behind for hours upon hours, only to come home, exhausted and cranky, and have to make dinner, tidy the house, and then be kept up at night by children and whatever germs they brought home from daycare that week.

It's not the working that's the problem – we like to and want to work; it's the job itself that doesn't work anymore. It was fine before the kids, when there was a lot of downtime and we could recharge and relax during our off hours. There were ways to make it okay and, for a long time, it didn't seem like nearly enough of a big deal to change things. The money was good. The vacation time was okay. The perks were lovely. There wasn't much to complain about – except maybe the one tiny detail that it increasingly become a Soul-sucking, unhappy place to work.

Having a baby made going there harder. There was this cute face and fluffy bottom to say goodbye to each day and that got harder and harder to do, instead of easier and easier like we'd expected. We get rather attached to the drooling, smiling, poop factories of awesome that we call our kids, and the last thing we wanted to do was leave them behind to go do things that were... well, less than wonderful. Leaving them wasn't fun, but we had to keep on going. Because money. And because sometimes we're just not too sure what else we want to be doing instead.

Decisions get harder when exhaustion plays such a big role in life, and while we can see the benefits of making a career change, we're not really sure how to pull it off. What if there's more schooling involved? Or having to learn about starting a business? We can't even fathom how to accomplish that *enormous* feat on the small amount of energy and sleep we're getting. A project that big definitely feels like something that should be saved for later... like maybe when the kids are married and have kids of their own.

Exhausted is the new normal. It's not that the kids are especially difficult or that there's anything we mind doing for them, but the relentlessness of each day, the interrupted sleep, the demands of each item on the to-do list, the unexpected things that pop up... well, it wears on a person. There's not a lot of time or energy left over at the end of the day, it seems.

And really, why rock the boat now? So we're bored and miserable at work – what's the big deal anyway? Lots of people are, after all. There are a few weeks vacation, some money, and you know exactly what you're getting each day. There's comfort in the familiarity. If it didn't steal our Souls and make us weep with boredom to go to work and try and fit in with Charlie from accounting and Louise from purchasing, we'd love our jobs, really we would. Probably. Okay, maybe not.

With such amazing perks, like being close enough to Starbucks to grab coffee a few times a day, and having a parking spot with our names on it, we really *should* be okay working there. We *should* take the steady, even road for the sake of the family. We *should* love the security and comfort of going there each day and knowing what to expect. We *should* want to keep a job that we worked so hard to get. We *should* feel good each day instead of feeling irritable and ready to snap when we get home. We *should* be in love with life and happy to live it each day. After all, we have what so many people want: a job, an awesome family, and a home to love.

Why ask for more?

Because you can be grateful for it all – every single bit of it – and still want more.

And that's okay.

* * *

There are costs to living an unsatisfying life and wanting each day to end, waiting for the weekend before we can begin to feel happy and satisfied, living only for the weekend. There are costs to not loving what we do.

There's the drain on our energy – working somewhere we don't want to be exhausts and drains us even more than working more hours doing something we love.

There's the drain on our emotional health – we choose to numb down our dissatisfaction by doing other things, such as Netflix and wine. Chocolate cake. Exercising too much. Sex. Retail therapy. Facebook. Pinterest. Housework. Projects or hobbies we take on but don't really love. And so on.

Refusing to feel how stressed and unhappy we are affects our health and wellness. We end up getting sick more often. Feeling more run down. Having extra headaches, soreness, weird lingering pain from injuries. We end up feeling like there's a big ol' heap of *blah* and *meh* blanketing our lives.

There's a drain in our ability to be happy and present moms – we find that weekends are the only time we get to be with our families without feeling too tired and cranky to deal with them.

When we really want to do something but we're not letting ourselves explore the options, we take up valuable thinking space – which is draining. We've *thought* ourselves into a giant tangled mess of "when that happens" …. "but not until that happens" …. "which can't happen until that other thing happens." And, so far, even though our minds have been up at night going over it and over it, we haven't been able to think up a solution.

What we're doing is looking for permission to do something wonderful for ourselves – even if it's terrifying and we're pretty sure we would fail. The good news is that this book is that permission.

* * *

Frazzled to Free outlines a framework of tools to help you get from where you are now to living the vision of Soul freedom that you desperately want and need. The journey includes learning how to tackle those fears.

- Chapter 1 – My Story. See how I used the framework to gain freedom.
- Chapter 2 – Your Shiny New Toolkit. Discover the tools that will get you there.
- Chapter 3 – Soul-Care. Learn how to care for yourself during the transition.
- Chapter 4 – Find Your Gifts. Relearn who you are now that you're a momma
- Chapter 5 – Divine Discontent. Clarify what you don't want.
- Chapter 6 – Dream That Dream. Envision your career and what you want to do next.
- Chapter 7 – Declare It. Clearly state your intentions
- Chapter 8 – Pull It Off. Discover how to get it done.
- Chapter 9 – The Obstacles. The stuff gets in the way and how to get around it.
- Chapter 10 – The Plan. Putting it all together.

You'll learn how to go from where you are right now to where you want to be: a fiercely happy momma with a shiny new career that makes your Soul sing and gives you the time you want with your family.

CHAPTER 1

My Story

"The best way out is always through."
– Robert Frost

I have had not one, but two-and-a-half career rock-bottoms. I am not one of those people who can nonchalantly work somewhere that isn't right for them. I have found it impossible to work in jobs that don't line up with me, my gifts, and my passions and my purpose in this world.

But it hasn't always been this way.

Rock Bottom 1.0

I had my career direction figured out at fifteen years old: I wanted to be a psychologist.

I remember a conversation I had with a friend of mine in the atrium of my high school. It was basically me ranting about everything I didn't want in a job once I was out of that place and into the grown-up world. My list went something like this:

- no windowless offices with ugly fluorescent lights
- no cubicles
- no long, boring hours doing crappy office work I hated
- no water cooler moments trading inane stories and small talk

Instead, I wanted the freedom of choosing my own hours in a bright and sunny office, with plants that I would probably kill often and have to replace. I was going to be a psychologist and help people figure out their problems. It was going to be *glorious*!

I followed that plan… for a while. I went to school for less than two years before I started to have a really hard time. Living on my own, working, and going to school were harder than I'd expected. I ended up really depressed, felt awful about not succeeding as well as I'd wanted to, and decided to quit.

Lost and unsure about what to do, I ended up finding a job that included every single item on that list I'd made in high school of what I didn't want. It somehow seemed like the easiest way forward.

I did Soul-crushing jobs for about five years before I just couldn't do it anymore. I couldn't stay working in those jobs for one more day. I was exhausted, numb, depressed, and felt like I was screaming on the inside. I had headaches and couldn't remember what it was like to feel happiness or joy. I needed to figure out a way out of it… and fast.

I called in sick to work, sat down on my back deck in the sunshine with my journal a book on figuring out careers, and got busy. I was going to fix that mess.

I didn't know it at the time, but the answers I got from trying to fix the mess came right from my Soul-self. I realized that no matter how many jobs I tried in reception or accounting, how many times I tried to finish my accounting certificate, or how many times I searched for another job that would magically make me feel happy and fulfilled but ultimately wouldn't, they were never going to work out for me. All of those jobs were going to feel like Soul-sucking, depression-creating awfulness – because they were all *very* wrong for me.

My sunshiny deck Soul-finding session ended with me remembering that kind of work I'd always wanted to do in this world: help others and be of service. I'd always wanted to become a psychologist and so I decided to dig around some more into career options similar to psychology and discovered life coaching as a career. Something clicked for me then.

I remember the moment of joy when I looked at the words written in my notebook. I swear, angels sang… or maybe it was my neighbor's car stereo. Regardless, there was music, and I'm sure it was meant just for me. I'd figured it out!

But since I was 25 and feeling a sense of urgency, because I wanted babies and was starting to consider what my life with kids would look like, and because I wanted my *shiny new career* as fast and as easily as possibly, I chose to *not* do the exact things my Soul told me to do. Why? Because I let fear and the obstacles in my way win.

I told myself that no one would hire a 25-year-old life coach. I reminded myself that I'd already tried and failed at school. I told myself it was dumb to sign up for another five or more years of school. Also, I had no idea how to start and run a business. I told myself all kinds of things that steered me away from what I'd just clarified that I truly wanted. I ended up with a big long list of reasons why it didn't make sense for me to do the scary things I'd have to do to go in the direction my Soul was pointing me.

So I looked at other options that would involve helping people: massage therapist, holistic health practitioner, acupuncturist, nutritionist.... all of them with short education times. All of them seeming less scary and more attainable. Safer. I decided on massage therapy.

I know. I know. Why would I do that to myself? Because it seemed *easier* and it seemed like it would be *good enough*. After all, I *loved* getting massages – being in the calm room, listening to soothing music – and I would be helping people soothe aches and pains. Wouldn't that be almost exactly the same as what I would be doing as a life coach or psychologist?

Nope. It wouldn't.

Rock Bottom 2.0

I knew massage therapy training was wrong for me in my first couple of months at massage school. I might have even known the second I walked in the door. But I wasn't listening to that wise part of me. I was telling myself that since the alternative was awful office jobs if I failed at massage school, I had to make this work... or else. I told myself that this was *good enough* and that I ought to shut my gob hole and learn how to soothe those aching muscles, because something needed to go well in my life.

So I learned to soothe those muscles. And I liked it more than an office job. But, truthfully, I didn't care much about the clients' carpal tunnel or frozen shoulders or whiplash. What I really wanted to know what was going on in their heads, hearts, and Souls. *Why* were they so stressed? What could they do to fix that? How did they feel about their marriages and bank accounts and their estranged children? I wanted to *talk* to them about their lives, not fix their neck pain.

But I didn't know that with clarity at that time. All I knew was that being a massage therapist wasn't feeling much better for me, after all, than working at an office job. I didn't connect the dots about *why* massage wasn't working out for me right then. I learned about that later.

All through massage school, I still worked at my office job, while trying to find the courage to make the leap into finding a part-time massage job to build up a clientele. To keep myself in place, I used excuses like "self-employment is hard" and "I want kids soon, so I'd better keep working at this crappy office job so that I can qualify for maternity leave" and "I really like stealing stationery supplies, so I might as well keep working here.". I didn't look deeper into my excuses. I just felt frustrated that I couldn't seem to get past them.

After some major bumps in that road, I managed to graduate from massage school with a diploma in remedial massage. I immediately felt *lost*.

I thought there was something wrong with me because I wasn't jumping up and down with excitement to start my new career. After all, I'd spent a couple years learning a skill I thought I wanted to do for a job – so why couldn't I do it already?

Frustrated with myself, I would sit at my desk at work and search for careers for hours! I was seriously the fastest hole puncher and paper filer ever, so I could take time to look online at *everything* career related. I looked at university programs and courses. I took quiz after quiz, personality assessment after assessment, trying to find answers to why I was so damned stuck. I thought that maybe looking at programs and doing assessment could help me figure myself out and something would magically click and whisper "dooooo thiiiiiiissssss, it's perrrrrrrfeeeeect for yooooooou."

My Soul had already whispered to me, but I'd ignored it.

Soul Nudges

After graduation from massage school, while I was still working at an office job, I did a quiz from the Government of Canada that told me to go be a psychic for a living. At the time, I thought it was hilarious that the government thought that anyone could make money from that kind of work. *Yeah, right,* I thought. *Why would anyone sign up for that? Crappy pay and dealing with crazy people all the time. People would be insane to want that.*

But that sneaky government was onto something. They had zeroed in on something I'd forgotten about myself: I really do have amazing intuition. It's one of my gifts, and it's one that I didn't use in office work, but that I would in doing coaching or counselling. At the time, I wasn't able to see that, though. I was ignoring the Soul nudges, partly because I wasn't comfortable with the answers I was getting from them, and partly because they didn't make sense to me. It was like getting tiny pieces of a puzzle but not being able to see what they meant or to do more with them until more pieces were available.

So I kept on looking and searching.

All that searching and no easy answers appeared for me. For the fourth or fifth time in my life, I fell into a job related depression. It was much like the other times: full of stuckness, lethargy, lack of interest in much of anything, irritability, excessive frustration, and anger.

My failed attempts at a career change were dragging me down to a new rock bottom.

But this time was a bit different, because I'd been reading self-help books and really trying to figure out a deeper solution to my problems. I decided to try something else. Instead of stuffing down my unhappiness, I leaned into it.

I let myself feel it. I let myself be anti-social and complain and whine and generally be miserable. And then magic things began to happen and, eventually, I started to feel better. I started to take some classes, I read more self-help books, I cleared out my life.

As the depression eased more and more of life started to feel good again, I felt ready to step into being a massage therapist and really give it a try. I came up with a plan to open a home-based massage business while working at my office job. I would dip my toes into the massage world and see what I thought. Take it slow.

Then I got pregnant and my big plan fell apart. It was the best thing to have ever happened to me!

The good news was that the decision to move forward with massage as my only job was decided for me the moment "Pregnant" appeared on the pregnancy tests (all six of them).

I was immediately horrified at the thought of going back to work full-time at a Soul-sucking office job while leaving my little one at home. I knew I would probably get used to it, if given the chance, but something in me that didn't want that. I wanted to be home with him more than a full-time job would allow. I'd always wanted that.

My baby boy arrived and, in my mind, I transformed from a woman into a mom. Maternity leave with him was both the best (baby snuggles!) and worst (sleeplessness) time, because it solidified my reasons for finding work that allowed me to be home with him and any other children I would end up having. I was ready to get rid of my office job once and for all.

I got to work creating my massage business and setting up a massage space in my home. I decided it was going to be amazing and unicorns were going to dance around and there was going to be glitter everywhere. I had my son, I had a wedding to plan, and I had stars in my eyes. Life was going to be wonderful!

But then... it wasn't. I mean, it was, because I had my son and my husband, whom I adored, but I started my massage business thinking all my problems were going to be solved by it.

Except for the one big elephant in the room: I still didn't much care for the actual job. I was proficient enough in my skills, though, and my business grew steadily enough over that time. I didn't enjoy the business side of my business – marketing and spreadsheets and office work and whatnot. Seeing clients was the best part. I enjoyed talking with them, but that wasn't enough. I often felt frustrated that we weren't getting to the heart of their issues, that massaging their knots wasn't the best way for me to be working with them.

In the back of my mind, there was always a lingering desire to be a psychologist or life coach, but, by that point, I was too busy with my family to consider a change that big. Between the fears I still had and the busyness of my life, big change didn't seem possible for me. It seemed like something I would do later in life, after life calmed down or my kids were in school.

So, I took more massage courses and tried to make the best of the massage and office skills I already had. I thought it would be selfish to train for *yet another* career when I'd spent so much time and energy getting what I already had. It was still *good enough*.

I felt too invested to pull the plug on my massage business outright, so I found a sneaky way around having to admit that my business wasn't doing it for me and probably never would.

I wanted a second baby. I thought, *Kayla, you should shut down your massage business to go back to an office job and get yourself some hours for a second maternity leave so you wouldn't have to work at all for a while. How bad could it be?* It sounded pretty reasonable to me, since there would be an end date to the office work, and a baby to cuddle at the end, so I did that. I temporarily closed down my massage business, and it felt good to me. Like, really, really good. I know now that it felt so good because that career was wrong for me.

For the first two months of the new office job, it was nice to be around other people again as a colleague. There were people to chat with. I got a steady amount of money each payday just for showing up and shuffling paper around. I had benefits. And then, suddenly, it became beyond awful. Backstabbing co-workers, absent bosses, my beloved manager left, and my foolproof plan wasn't so delightful anymore. In fact, it was like being picked up from a warm sunny place and then thrown down a cold, dark pit of despair and woe.

Rock Bottom 2.5

A few months in to my office adventure, when I started to realize that not only did massage not work for me, but the peaceful work and steady income I'd expected at my old office job had become *awful*. I wasn't pregnant yet, couldn't quit, and it dawned on me that I had gotten myself stuck in between a rock and a hard place. This was the start of my last time of hitting rock bottom.

One day, after realizing that I was incredibly unhappy with both the career options I thought I had, I went out for an extra-long lunch and tried to find something in the bookstore (my happy place) to make me feel better. I believe I even requested/prayed to find something that would make everything feel okay again. I came across a book that was a game-changer for me: *Finding Your Own North Star*, by Martha Beck. I read it in a day. After finishing, I went to Google to find out more about Martha. Amazingly enough, she had a training program for *life coaches*!

I began to have crazy thoughts that maybe, just maybe, I really could be a life coach. My north star was pointing right to it, after all. That is when I started to finally listen to what my Soul had been telling me for so long. And, because I did, I started to find my way.

From there, things started happening. Serendipitous things. Like, a blogger I followed offered coaching sessions in her newsletter, and she happened to be a Martha Beck-trained life coach. So I signed up to try it. I was terrified. But, I swear, angels sang again.

The life coaching sessions I did fascinated me. I loved it! They made me realize that I wanted to be the one doing the coaching. I got really brave one day and decided to leap right in: I signed up for the Martha Beck Life Coach training program.

A month later, I found myself pregnant with my second child. It was all lining up.

It seemed like it was all going to be easy, with unicorns and singing angels again, but all kinds of obstacles came up. We had house renovations to do before the baby came. I was working a lot of hours to save up some money for maternity leave and beyond. I was so very sick through my whole pregnancy, and the timing for the worst of my morning sickness was right when the coaching training calls were.

But I showed up anyway. Or I listened to the recordings later. But I made it happen this time, and I got through it. I learned how much I could handle without breaking when what I was doing was important to me. That challenging time has become my new threshold for cataclysms– nothing so far has been as crazy as that year of pregnancy/renovation/coaching training.

Another obstacle I faced was my belief in myself. With being so sick during my pregnancy, I didn't show up the way I wanted on the training calls. I was *there* each time, but I rarely spoke, and my exhaustion levels kept me from reaching out and practicing as much as I wanted and needed to. That left me with a confidence issue. Since I hadn't practiced enough, I didn't think I was able to coach, so I didn't. Which is funny, because asking for more help and practicing more were the only ways to get better. I shot myself in my own foot there. Again.

With my lack of belief in myself firmly entrenched, I went back to doing massages after the coach training ended, planning to do both, but really only focusing on massage. I thought it was the easier path (do you see a theme here yet?) to do what was familiar instead of trusting in my new skills as a coach or practicing to get better. I believed I had to be an expert right away. I believed no one would want to work with me yet. I believed so many things – including a bunch of old, fearful beliefs that had held me back for years; the ones already in place when I chose massage over coaching or psychology.

So I did massage and worked on my coaching business with two young kids to mother and a home to keep running. It was a recipe for disaster and I found myself staring burnout and depression in the eyes again.

But, this time, when those signs of depression kicked in, I had my handy dandy new skills as a life coach to use. I had learned to listen to my body's wisdom. I was *finally* in tune with myself enough to recognize the problems I was having for what they were.

I realized that when I'm on the wrong path, my body throws depression at me as a way to get my attention. It creates a combination of restlessness energy, frustration, anger, listlessness, and lethargy. It does this faster and with more ferocity as time goes on – as if my body is impatient with my inability to see what's in front of me. The faster I see, the faster I can course-correct and not get bogged down in thinking that I need to slow down or stop everything. The problems and answers for me are rarely what I first believe they are; instead, they usually require deeper inquiry at the Soul level to get to the bottom of them.

It Takes Courage

It takes a whole lot of courage to live from the Soul and take a leap from things that are *good enough* and to move into *amazing*. It takes courage to look backward and see that the lessons were there all the time. It takes courage to take a stand and go all-in for what you really want, even when it's scary. It takes courage to go looking for truth, and to look within for answers.

I found out all of this when I decided to take a chance and enroll in Soul's Calling coach training right after maternity leave with my second son was over. In that training, I learned all about my gifts, who I am, and what I want. Best of all, I met my Soul.

I knew there were things I did well, but I had never considered them to be gifts. I thought "gifts" were things like a natural talent for music or painting. I didn't think my sense of humor, my leadership ability, my ability to inspire, my love for teaching, my ability to see both the big and small pictures and break things down into manageable chunks, or my ability to really see people for who they truly are were gifts. I couldn't even *see* those parts of me at all. It wasn't until I spent time at a retreat in Mexico with other women during the training that I really got it.

Meeting My Soul

I formally met my Soul – that old, wise part of me; my guide; my compass – on a sandy beach in the Mayan Riviera. It was two days into a four-day retreat where we dove deep into getting to know ourselves and our gifts. We had a free afternoon so I decided to sit on the beach and do a meditation. With the sounds of the ocean, conversations going on around me, and people playing in the ocean, along with the work we had been doing in the days before, it all lined up just right for my Soul to come out and play.

I met her and it changed everything instantly. As crazy as it sounds, a ten-minute meditation in the right time and place and with the right people opened me up and created space for every brave and crazy thing I did then and continue to do now. Knowing her has made all the difference.

It was meeting this part of myself that gave me the courage to swim in the ocean for the first time. I'd always been *terrified* of the ocean. I had never dipped more than a toe in it before. But on this trip, in the company of those women, I pulled off the bravest thing I have ever done besides giving birth twice: I went snorkeling with sea turtles.

It's no joke when I say that my biggest fear is open water and not being able to touch the ground in water. But, that day, with my Soul-self, I put on the flippers. And then the mask. And then, amazingly enough, and even though my chest was shaking with fear and panic and I could barely breathe or speak, I let myself be led into deeper water by Diego, our guide. Even more amazing, I actually put my face in the water, tingling with fear, and opened my eyes to see a sea turtle right in front of me! She was the most beautiful thing I have ever laid eyes on (besides my children the moment they were put on my chest all red-faced and gooey). I found myself moving deeper into the water to see more turtles. And then more fish. By the end, I didn't even need Diego anymore, I was moving and swimming along *on my own*. In the big, beautiful, scary *ocean*!

By the time we got back to the beach, I was calm. I had just conquered my biggest fear and it felt like a religious experience. I wasn't able to describe it or talk about it for quite some time, but that feeling became my new touchstone for "feeling the fear and doing it anyway."

The year after that Mexico retreat was the most transformative year of my life. I'd met my Soul, learned to listen to my body's wisdom, felt my feelings, and was tuning in more and more to what everything in my mind, body, and Soul was telling me.

I was finally listening.

Taking The Leap

I quit my massage business for the second and final time when I *finally* (cue the applause) started to connect the dots that what was wrong with massage was massage itself. It would never be my work because my work isn't with my hands on clients to ease their pain and suffering. My work is with my ability to speak and connect with them about their thoughts, beliefs, and dreams. It's my ability to see them and to see the parts of the problem they can't, and use the tools I've learned to help them find answers that are right for them.

I went full steam ahead into my coaching business. I've also spent my time gathering the lessons I learned over the past decade on why I didn't follow my Soul's nudges. I've packed those lessons into a framework that will help others along on their own path to finding the (so far) elusive meaningful work they crave.

Meet Ellie

Ellie found herself in a similar situation to mine when her daughter was born. She was working as a nurse at a hospital that was across the city, making for a long commute. It was a pretty good job and she was really comfortable with her work and her co-workers, so she didn't see herself leaving it.

The trouble was that nursing, no matter how comfortable a position it was overall, wasn't doing it for her. She often found herself bored and frustrated by her job, even though she didn't want to feel that way. She loved taking courses and learning, and found herself enrolling in a massage therapy program, which she absolutely fell in love with. Massage was along the same helping and caring lines as nursing, Ellie thought the switch wouldn't make much of a difference to her happiness level, but it did.

As time went on and she fell more in love with massage, she decided to cut her nursing hours down so she could do both nursing and massage therapy, but she talked herself into staying in nursing part-time, even though her heart wasn't in it anymore. When her son was diagnosed with autism, she realized that the long commute to her nursing job was getting in the way of her peace of mind, since she worried so much when she was so far away from him.

After an especially difficult time with her son being sick and no one else being able to care for him, she decided that, for her son, she had to take the plunge and quit nursing, even though it made her incredibly sad to leave that position behind after a decade. She mourned her old job, but also felt a huge boost to her happiness when she concentrated on massage more full-time and was more available for her son when her needed her. As time went on, she became more and more *thrilled* with the change. In the end, she wasn't sure why she'd stayed in nursing as long as she had.

Ellie and I didn't do Soul work together until a while later. When we did, she saw exactly why her nursing job, although good enough, wasn't ever going to be what made her come alive. She also saw how life intervened on her behalf and created a way for her to quit her job and move into work that lights her up. It all worked out for the best.

Interestingly enough, the exact work I was called to move away from is the work that calls to Ellie most. This goes to show that we all have our unique gifts and callings that, when we answer, are exactly right for us.

My Soul's Calling

It's wondrous to me how often having children is the catalyst for not only becoming a new person (becoming a mom), but also for other big changes, such as a new career or job. There is a wonderful and quiet but fierce strength that starts to flow once we're left in charge of a new life, and this strength can be, and often is, harnessed and turned into amazing things – like choosing to follow one's Soul and create new career or job opportunities. Doing this is not only *for* our kids, to set an example for them of finding the courage and energy to make those things happen, but *because* we have them in our lives.

Coaching and writing are my current Soul's callings. This is a career that takes my gifts and my passion for helping mommas find work that makes them come alive, and mashes them together in ways that make me feel alive, happy, and fulfilled.

The more I look back and see the Soul nudges that were there but ignored, the more I appreciate and am grateful for the gentle Soul guide that is a huge, and probably the most important, part of who I am. In looking back, I see a pattern that emerges to provides the framework for this book and the process I learned and that I now use with my clients.

I can see exactly where I turned away from the right path and *why* I did it. I can see the beliefs and fears I had that kept me from becoming a life coach, even though I knew, way back when, that that was exactly what I wanted and needed to be. I can see all the bumps in the road, all the obstacles, and all the ways I turned away from what I needed.

I can see it for others as well. The intuition I was ignoring back when the Government of Canada told me to be a psychic comes in handy in my work now. I can see the paths forward for my clients. I can see the bumps in the road for them. Most, or even all, of my formerly seemingly random gifts, skills, and talents have magically merged together in this life coaching and writing path.

Here is the framework of steps, which I will cover in more detail in the remainder of this book, to get from a career that is no longer working to one that will. The first step is to get still and free your Soul so you can get to know what those quiet but persistent nudges look like. Next is to really get to know your gifts and own them with confidence. From there, take a look at the life you have and the life you want and find ways that work for you and your family to bridge the gap. In the process, get to know and learn to overcome the obstacles that rise up along the way. Yes, there will be some. That's okay, because we are kind but fierce Soul seekers who are ready to win at life.

CHAPTER 2

Your Shiny New Toolkit

"Whatever's good for your Soul.... Do that."
–Unknown

One of the things that a lot of traditional career assessments and tools leave out is actually the biggest and most important piece of the puzzle: your beautiful Soul.

I spent years and years looking outside for answers and it got me two career paths that didn't work for me. Only by looking within instead of searching outside did I discover the right path.

I believe that the same goes for you as well. Looking within will get you the answers you need – answers that fill that quiet void within that's been a little bit (or a lot) dissatisfied with life and your current job, no matter how good it looks from the outside. Answers from your Soul fill that ache and move you toward work that is meant just for you, work that will fill you up and bring more meaning and satisfaction into your life.

From now on, the first step to any question that comes up for you will be to get still, listen for answers from your Soul, and then lead from the Soul – no matter how crazy the answer seems.

Free Your Soul

So, what is your Soul anyway? Your Soul is the deepest, wisest, most knowing part of you. Freeing your Soul opens up the doorway to getting to know your most alive, most loving, and most grounded self – the self that is authentic, open, honest, and living on purpose, instead of mired in seeking answers from outside sources and wanting the approval of others.

Living from the Soul is choosing to live from your highest purpose. It is listening within and living your own truth, not what's easy or convenient or what others want for you. It is choosing love everyday – love for yourself, love for your life, and love for the gifts you have been given. It is doing the hard things for the right reasons and coming out the other side with more than you could have imagined. Living from the Soul means going right into the muck and yuck to find the richness there, getting through it, and coming out stronger and better on the other side.

Living from your Soul is a beautiful thing.

Why do we want to free our Souls? In her book *Meet Your Soul*, Elisa Romero answers that question: "Because your Soul is the oldest, wisest, and always-loving part of yourself, and She has access to incredible knowledge. Your Soul knows why you came to the planet, what lesson you most need to learn, and how to perfectly navigate and heal the challenges in your life."

You're thinking that if it's so good to be living from the Soul, why aren't we all doing just that? The truth is that is takes a lot of bravery to live Soulfully. It takes a lot of courage to live your life truly as yourself and for yourself. To follow the nudges and crumbs that the Soul leaves for us, we often have to do things that are uncomfortable and go to places within ourselves that need healing. This isn't the easiest thing to do and often we turn away from that work.

We turn away in many different ways – binge-watching Netflix, drinking too much, eating too much, numbing out with technology, shopping, sex, exercise, working too much – and we ignore the signs from our Souls that are guiding us to live more Soulfully. It may feel easier to live separated from the Soul, but then there is often a sense of dissatisfaction and unrest underneath our choices.

Amazing things happen when we move away from the easy-seeming choices and, instead, choose to live from the Soul outward. Doors open up in odd but fantastic new ways. Synchronicities happen. Things line up, fall apart, and then line up again even better than we could have imagined. It's a beautiful dance.

Learning to tap into the Soul for clues toward work that is meaningful is the beginning of a long and beautiful relationship.

What stands in our way of living from the Soul? A whole lot.

When we are born, we are fully ourselves. Until we learn to not be, that is. The expectations of our parents, teachers in school, our friends, people around us – they all change us. We change ourselves and mold ourselves to fit in. We pack ourselves into tiny little boxes with labels and learn to listen to others for what is best for us, so that we're not labeled as weird or different, so we can fit in with the teachings of our parents, schools, and churches.

We keep the "acceptable" bits of ourselves and toss the "unacceptable" bit out and into our shadow, which is where we stuff those undesirable parts and the parts of ourselves we deny. We don't allow ourselves the chance to fully be who we truly are. And a lot of the time, we don't even realize we're doing it.

Our real Soul selves are inside; it just takes some uncovering to get all the pieces back, which is partly what this book is about – letting our Soul selves out to shine, gathering up all the bits that we've tossed into our shadows, and using them as a guide to work that is of service and meaningful to us.

Ellie (who you met in Chapter 1), while attending one of my Women's Circles where we discuss the gifts that we have that we don't recognize, got very excited when the topic of intuition came up. She had experienced a lot of psychic abilities while she was growing up, and so had others in her family. Both her grandma and her father regularly talked about it and having psychic abilities was a big part of Ellie's life. But, as she got older, with the pressures of fitting in at school and not wanting to be considered "weird," she let it drop away; she lost that part of herself. It wasn't until our Women's Circle that night that she connected with that lost part of herself and started to learn to embrace it again.

Soul Nudges

You know that inane chatter in your mind that narrates your day and won't shut up? Yeah, that's not your Soul's voice. Your mind talks to you using language while your Soul speaks to you in more abstract ways. This is exactly why it's so easy to keep listening to mind chatter and not find or listen to the ways your Soul is communicating with you.

That feeling of "just knowing" when something is wrong or "just knowing" when someone good is about to happen. That feeling of excitement as an opportunity presents itself. The sensation of familiarity and joy when you smell something that reminds you of your childhood or hear a song that takes you back. That sinking sensation when something is about to go wrong. Those are all your Soul Voice communicating with you. I call these things Soul nudges or Soul crumbs – you'll see both those terms used interchangeably.

Soul nudges are how your Soul tells you that something is a hot track for you, something you should pursue.

* * *

We've talked about how I am an intuitive person, but ignored that part of me for a long time. I used to live on an acreage (with my now ex) where we had a whole zoo – four cats and four dogs. One day, three of our dogs ran away. Two of them were constantly doing it, so it wasn't a surprise and they always came back, but what was surprising is that the third dog, Foxy, who was a timid little thing who followed the rules, went with them. We searched *everywhere* for them. Eventually, the next day, the two who normally went adventuring came back, but Foxy was still missing. We decided to go driving around to look for her. A few range roads down and one over, I felt this urge to stop. But, since there was a car coming up behind us, only slowed down and called out the window, trying to see Foxy's golden fur in a field of golden wheat. We didn't actually stop and get out of the car. She didn't come when we called for her. Disappointed, we went home to eat before going out to search again.

While we were eating, we got a call telling us that someone had Foxy. She had been hiding out in the barn with their dogs for most of the day and they'd just discovered her. It turned out that their son had thought that they'd gotten a new dog when he saw her that morning and they'd "forgotten" to tell him the truth, since Foxy had seemed so at home. We followed the directions to their house and it was *exactly* where I'd felt that urge to stop earlier in the day. Only, since we hadn't thought she would be hiding in a barn that was *kilometers* from her home, we didn't check out the house that was at the end of a long driveway where we'd slowed down.

If I had not disowned and ignored my gift of intuition and had been able to listen to the hit of Soul nudging when I got it on that dirt road, we could have saved ourselves a night of worry and sleeplessness.

Free Your Soul – Step 1: Get to Know Your Body Guide

Grab a pad of paper and a pen handy in case you want to write down anything after doing this exercise.

Your body is a beautiful work of art. It allows you to move, dance, and hug your kids. It is also the means by which your Soul will most frequently communicate with you. The more you get in touch with what your body is telling you, the easier it is to listen to Soul.

You learn to do this by learning what the sensations in your body are telling you.

Sit comfortably in a chair. Take a few deep belly breaths. Feel yourself relaxing. Feel your shoulders begin to drop. Feel your throat open up. Feel your jaw relax. Keep breathing. Notice your eyes – do they feel heavy? Close them for a moment and just breathe.

Think of a time in your life when things weren't going so hot. Not the worst time in your life – don't go there! But pick a time when you weren't happy. Imagine it carefully. Now notice what's happening to your body as you think of this. What sensations do you feel? Where do you feel them? What's happening to you?

Write it down. Write everything you felt in your body as you remembered that unhappy time, from where you felt it to what it felt like. Get creative. Really describe what you felt and where you felt it. How bad did you feel, on a scale of -1 to -10 (minus 1 to minus 10)?

Shake that memory off. Get back into your relaxed state. Now go to a time where you felt terrified about something that ended up being amazing for you. You felt scared and unsure, but it ended up being a good thing in your life. Maybe it was a job opportunity you were unsure about, maybe it was a blind date, or something else entirely. Notice what's happening to your body when you think of this. What sensations do you feel? Where do you feel it? What's happening to you?

Write it down. Write everything, from where you felt it to what it felt like. Get creative. Really describe what you felt and where you felt it. How did you feel on a scale of -1 to +10?

Shake it off. Move your body around and take some deep breaths. Then get back into your relaxed state again – relaxed from your fingers to your toes to your hips to the top of your head. Relax. Release. Breathe. Breathe deeply three to five times or so, clearing your mind to think of nothing but your breath.

Think of a time in your life when things were amazing. You were happy and joyful and living was easy. It can be a really good time in your life, but not the best. Imagine it carefully. Really get into it. Notice what's happening to your body when you think of that time. What sensations do you feel? Where do you feel them? What's happening to you?

Write it down. Write everything, from where you felt it to what it felt like. Get creative. Really describe what you felt and where you felt it. How good did you feel on a scale of +1 to +10?

Take a few deep breaths and shake that memory off, too. Move around. Dance. Return to yourself.

* * *

You now have a very important tool at your disposal. At times, things in life *seem* like a really good idea, but if you were to check in with your body, you would quickly find out that rather than feeling thrilled about it, you were actually getting a negative body guide reading. That means that no matter how amazing that opportunity is, it's not right for you.

Something like a job promotion or a new career option may seem to you and others to be the best move forward for you, but if you're getting any body sensations that read more on the negative scale than on the positive, it's not really right for you. You can say no and thus open the door for an opportunity that is right for you to come along.

Practice this tool and you'll get better and better at it. The key to this tool, especially when it seems like you're getting false readings to something, is to break the things you're asking your body for a Soul reading about into smaller chunks.

If you're trying to use this tool to tell whether or not you should quit your job, but you keep getting different readings, break what you're asking down and get a reading on each smaller part.

You might find that quitting your job has a super high positive reading, but when you look at the money part of the decision you get a negative reading and realize you're afraid of losing your house if you quit your job. Now you know more specifically where the work for you is.

Once you've started practicing the body guide process, move on to practicing Step 2: Freeing Your Soul, which will help you learn to recognize and listen to your Soul's voice and to trust those Soul nudges. Trust is the key to building a beautiful, Soulful career and life.

Free Your Soul – Step 2: Meditation

Have a pad of paper and a pen ready to write anything down that you want to remember.

Take five deep belly breaths. Starting at your toes, imagine that they are being bathed in a beautiful, bright light. This light is filled with ease, peace, and relaxation. It moves up your feet to your ankles and up your legs. It reaches your hips and slowly moves up your belly to your heart. At each point, it pauses and radiates peace and ease for a moment before moving up. It moves further, to your shoulders, and then down your arms to the tips of your fingers and back up your arms to your neck and throat. It moves up the back of your head and down your face. Peace, ease, and relaxation settle in deeply. Take another deep breath, filling your belly. Release that breath slowly.

Imagine a tiny ball of light, about the size of a quarter, right between your eyes. Imagine it right at the front of your head, at the place where your mind chatters at you and where you feel the narrative of your day takes place. Move that light inward to the centre of your mind and let it rest there for a moment before seeing it move down your spine, lining up your chakras as it goes down. It then expands to the size of a baseball and the light continues to move down your spine slowly until it reaches your root chakra. Let the light shine back up to the top of your head. Breathe deeply. You are now bathed in light – inside and out. Breathe deeply here for a few breaths.

Turn your awareness to the edges of your skin. Feel the energy there. Expand that energy outward until it reaches a distance around your body equal to where the tips of your fingers would be if your arms were outstretched. Imagine your hands together and your arms raised above your head. Imagine your hands breaking apart and slowly moving down the sides of your body with your arms still stretched out while that energy moves with it, filling in the space all around you. Feel that bubble of your energetic space as you imagine your arms landing at your sides. Breathe for a moment and feel that space.

Your Soul is a part of you. It is both you and not you. It is the deepest, most knowing part of you. Now begin to focus your awareness inward and gently invite your Soul to meet you. Invite your Soul to fill that energetic space around you. Be patient. Let your Soul come to you slowly and be known.

Ask your Soul if it has any messages for you. Wait. Breathe. You may find that you are flooded with words, images, smells, sounds, memories, or you may find that there's only one piece to the message. Breathe. Allow it to come. You Soul might communicate with you in a variety of ways, or even not at all at this time. Everything is valid. Everything is okay.

Spend some time here for a few minutes, breathing gently in your own rhythm. Feel the energy bubble expand and contract with each breath you take. Let whatever needs to come up come up. If nothing does, *don't worry*, sometimes it takes a few tries to learn to sit in stillness and listen. Just sit and be open. Be curious.

If you received a message, send some gratitude to your Soul. Take another deep breath or two. And slowly come back.

Move your body in any way that feels good to you. Go for a walk. Jump. Run. Dance. Just move. Write down anything you discovered or learned. The more you do this simple meditation, the easier it will be to get to know your Soul.

* * *

I know that you didn't skip doing those meditations, that you did both of them and have now bonded completely with your Soul self, because you're awesome. But, because I also know it's hard to read a meditation and do it in a way that works well and that means it's so tempting to skip these steps, even though they are so important, I have recorded them for you as a gift (because I heart you). You can find them on my website: www.FrazzledToFreeBook.com/meditations.

If you experience resistance to doing this, it means, paradoxically, that your Soul definitely wants you to do it, because there's something important in there for you.

* * *

The first time Ellie did the meditation, she immediately exclaimed "Wow, I hadn't ever really thought about having a Soul and using it to find answers like that. I usually just pray."

Which leads me to my next point. If meditation isn't your thing, there are other ways to communicate with your Soul. Meditation is a great first step in creating the stillness and openness required to free your Soul, but prayer, journaling, walking, running, yoga, and creating art are some of the other ways of opening communication so that your Soul's nudges can come through. Some ways might be easier or harder for you. Experiment!

Let's look at a few of those other ways in a bit more detail now.

Journaling

You can practice hearing your Soul's voice by writing. Grab a journal and write a question for your Soul. It can be about *anything*. "Why do I love Michael Jackson so much?" or "What's my purpose?" or "Why does my car keep breaking down?" Find a meaningful question that you want answered and write it down.

Now switch the pen into your non-dominant hand, take a deep breath or two as you contemplate the question, and then write the first thing that comes to you. Don't worry if it doesn't make sense at first. Don't worry about feeling awkward or if your writing is messy. You're opening the channel of communication with your Soul. It takes focus and practice and time for you two to meet and become BFFs.

This method is essentially how the whole book series *Conversations With God* by Neale Donald Walsch was written.

Exercise

Bring up a question you want to ask and ask it before going for a run or doing yoga or any other activity during which your mind is fully occupied with the task and can't chatter away at you. Doing anything you enjoy and that makes time feel like it stops puts you in a space that's called "being in flow," and it is a beautiful thing.

An answer may come during the activity, afterward, or even, sometimes, days later. The key is to ask and then let go of thinking of the answer and let it come to you naturally, in its own time.

Create Art

It doesn't matter if you can paint like Bob Ross, bake like Betty Crocker, color like a two-year-old, or sculpt the best Play-Doh figurines; the act of working with your hands, asking your question, and then emptying your mind while occupied with the task of creating can get you your answers as well.

Free Your Soul – Step 3: Decide How You Want to Feel

The question "How do you want to feel?" from Danielle LaPorte changed my life. Really. It was one of the first times that it connected for me that I get to *choose* how I *feel* in my life. I have the power to move toward the things that make me feel good and away from the things that make me feel like garbage. That includes how I spend my time, who I spend it with, and when it happens. Game-changer.

It works the same way for you, too. You get to choose how you feel. You get to pick, out of all the ways to feel out there, which ones resonate the most with you, and choose to do the things that will move you closer to feeling that way.

Because wanting something really is about how the goal makes you feel in the end. We chase goals not because of the goal itself, but because of how reaching it will make us feel. It's not really about getting the Oscar; it's about feeling the pride, accomplishment, joy, and recognition of having done so. It's not really about getting the promotion; it's about feeling valued, and feeling satisfaction. It's really not about publishing a book; it's about feeling whole, and accomplished, feeling joy, creativity, and love.

When the going gets tough, and it usually does, it's pretty easy to get back on track by tuning tune in again to how you want to feel. That will get you back into that goal-getting head space. Why? Because you can choose how you want to feel right now. Today. This moment. Don't wait until you reach the goal – get the job, lose the weight, go on that vacation – to feel the way you want to feel. Go ahead and feel it now. What can you think or do right now to feel the way you want to feel when you've reached your goal?

Reaching that goal will bring *more* of those desired feelings, that's for sure, but since you can feel that way now, you don't have to wait. You don't have to wait to lose weight to feel beautiful. You don't have to get the job to feel accomplished. You don't have to wait for your kids to be older to feel peace. You can feel it all now. Reaching the goal is just the extra, delicious icing on the cake – but you do get to eat the cake along the way.

* * *

In a session with Anna, the mom of a one-year-old little boy, we talked about her desire to move to a new, smaller town that would work better for her and her family. Even though she wanted to make the move, she had so many fears around it. I asked her why she wanted to move and, when she answered, she sounded like she was reading from a phone book. She had answers all ready to go, as if she'd been listing them to herself all day long. And she probably had. Her mind had told her over and over again the reasons why she needed to move, even though it scared her.

She said, "We would be able to afford a larger home. We could afford more for our kids and my mom could come live with us if she needed to. We would feel safer. My husband's paycheck would go further...." She went on for a while, listing reasons.

When I asked her how she would feel once she had the house in the new town, her voice changed. It got lighter and more upbeat as she told me she would feel more like a grown-up who had arrived once they'd made the move and bought the bigger house. She would feel ease and playfulness. She would have friends over more often, because she loved to entertain and would have more space to do so. She would feel like she had more communion and community. She would feel more relaxed in her space, because everyone in her family would have a place of their own in the new house. The clutter would be gone and they would have more money to go around.

Rather than waiting for that magic day when she got the keys to her new home to feel all of those wonderful feelings, I asked her to consider ways she could feel those things now. She came up with a list of things she could do to bring more communion, community, ease, and playfulness into her life right away.

By the end of our call, Anna was in love with the ways she would feel in her new home and she happily went off to look at real estate listings to dream about what her new home could look like and to find ways to feel in the present how she wanted to feel when she was in the new house.

* * *

So, how do *you* want to feel? Take a look at your goals. What is the feeling behind the goals you thing about each day? The goals you want for your year? Your goals for each area of your life. How are you going to feel when you accomplish them?

Make a list of all the ways you want to feel in your life, broken down into any categories that make sense for you; for example: love, family, work, health, home, friendships, money.

Come up with a list of four of five words or phrases that really sum up how you want to feel in general in your life and use those as a theme for your goal setting and achieving.

Build your daily to-do list and monthly and yearly goals to fulfill that feeling intention, by asking yourself, "How do I want to feel, and will doing this get me closer or further away from that feeling?"

It's likely that how you want to feel will change as you go forward toward your goals. Take some time every year or every quarter to review your goals and the feelings your associate with them. The list of feelings below can help you get started:

- Happy
- Joyful
- Alive
- Vibrant
- Expansive
- Spacious
- Love
- Accomplished
- Gratitude
- Wanderlust

- Communion
- Vital
- Whole
- Jazzed
- Focused
- Flowing
- Present

Free Your Soul – Step 4: Feel Your Feelings

There's determining how you want to feel each day and then there's feeling the feelings you have when things happen. They're similar, and yet different, but oh so powerful when used together.

We have emotions all the time. It usually goes like this: something happens, we form an opinion about it, we think about it – using our past experiences, beliefs, and values as references – and then we feel emotions about it: event, thought, emotion. Generally, something has to happen before we feel emotions.

You see a picture of a dog that looks like the one you had as a kid and you immediately think of Spot and, boom, you've got some sadness. You think of some other memories of him and, boom, there's some happiness and joy. All from seeing the random picture.

We think of something or hear something and that sequence happens automatically, so emotions follow. That song comes on the radio and we're taken back to the summer of our first love; cue the wistful-happy-nostalgic-sad emotion combination. Someone compliments us; cue the humble happiness. Our babies giggle for the first time and here comes the pride and joy. Things happen; we feel things.

* * *

In her book *The Art of Empathy*, Karla McLaren says, "The idea that there are negative or positive emotions is a completely unempathic and unhelpful fallacy. Our deeply unfortunate tendency to divide emotions into positive and negative categories has dreadful consequences in our everyday lives." In truth, there aren't any such things as positive or negative emotions; they're all simply messengers.

McLaren also says, "Our emotional training is often insufficient and confusing (and even backwards), and subsequently, our emotional understanding tends to be low." Meaning that we often have no idea what emotion we're feeling because we were never taught to identify them, or we try so hard to not feel things we don't like and try even harder to only feel the ones we want to. We assign positive and negative labels to our emotions, not realizing that there is beauty and truth in every single one of them.

When I say that we can choose how we want to feel, I don't mean that we *only* feel happiness or joy in our life, but, instead, that we make choices that move us toward those overall feeling states. It's kind of like choosing themes. Danielle LaPorte's "How do you want to feel?" question, prompts us to choose our life "themes" such that, when looking forward and backward, we can see the results of our choices and see where we want to go in order to feel more like that.

Emotions are here to tell us something. Nothing more. Even the so-called bad emotions, like anger, sadness, frustration, and dislike, are nothing more than clues to help us decode what is behind them. Letting ourselves feel our emotions is about listening to these messengers.

* * *

We women, a lot of the time, are told that we're not allowed to feel anger. That nice girls don't rock the boat. That it's not nice to make a scene. That we need to be happy and pleasant because then people will like us more. It's pure garbage.

Anger is a messenger to us to show us that our boundaries have been crossed – by us or by others. Feeling it and questioning it gets us answers and information. It guides us. Nothing more.

Some of us have been told for pretty much our entire lives that we're not allowed to feel the things that we do feel, so we tend to stuff those feelings down, ignore them, shut them off. We don't know how to feel things.

So how does one begin to feel their emotions? By taking some time and practicing.

When you are feeling something, but aren't sure what you're feeling, or what to do about it, here's a process you can go through to practice feeling your feelings.:

1. Notice that you are feeling something. Notice what you were just thinking about or what was happening just before. Name the emotion. If you're not sure, call it one of the main four categories of *sad*, *glad*, *angry*, or *afraid*. Be as specific as you can, but also know that, with practice, this gets easier.

2. Focus on your body – where are you feeling this emotion? What sensations do you feel? Describe them as best as you can. Focus on the sensations as they move through you. Do they change? Do they stay the same?

3. How old do you feel? Is there an age that pops into your mind? Maybe a memory of a time you felt like this when you were younger? Just notice this – you don't have to do anything with it.

4. As you keep focusing on the feeling, you might find that it starts to lessen and dissipate, that there's nothing left to focus on. Or you might find that there's another wave of feeling right behind it that's the same again or slightly different. When there's nothing left to feel, that's how you know you're finished!

5. Yay! You've just felt your emotion all the way through!

6. Write down anything that came up as a realization, if you'd like.

You probably noticed a few things as you did this: 1) emotions don't last for long if you actually feel them; 2) it might have been intense, but you made it through; 3) it gets easier to do the more you do it.

* * *

I had a session recently with a client, Lana. She was feeling angry over a fight she was having with her neighbor about whether to make some changes to the outside of her home. She was having a hard time finding a solution to her problem because she was so angry. I asked her if she was letting herself feel angry or if she was trying to avoid it. She replied that she always tried to take the high road with anger and work through it with affirmations and positive thoughts.

To me, it sounded like she was avoiding her anger. I led Lana through the exercise above, having her feeling her anger in her body for three minutes. I set the timer and told her that she only had to feel it for a short period of time. She did, and about two minutes in, I could feel the shift as the anger started to dissipate and seemed less intense for her.

After thanking her anger and then releasing it, she felt amazing! She was also able to see a solution to her problem with her neighbor. By feeling the anger, she could see what was going on, what was important for her to hold on to, and what she could let go of.

She felt powerful and at peace with a conflict that had been ongoing for quite some time.

* * *

There is nothing wrong with feeling fear, anger, or sadness. In fact, they can be powerful allies to fuel big changes, like big career changes, if they are felt and the messages behind them are allowed to come through.

CHAPTER 3

Soul Care

*"Be strong enough to stand alone, smart
enough to know when you need help, and
brave enough to ask for it."*
–Mark Amend

To navigate changes (transitions) in life – big and small – we need to learn to ask for and receive help, learn to take care of ourselves in ways that will actually help, and learn how to cultivate compassion toward ourselves. This combination all together is what I call *Soul Care*.

What is a transition, exactly? It's anything that changes who you are or what you do, and that has a clear "before and "after." Some examples are the death of a person close to you, getting a new job, becoming a parent, graduating from school, losing a job, finding out you are ill, and so forth.

In her book *Finding Your Own North Star*, Martha Beck says, "Catalytic events (transitions) offer you a wonderful chance to rethink your life, because each destroys fundamental aspects of your self-definition. They make it necessary for you to chart a new course through life, and they free you to find your essential (Soul) self, consult your internal compasses, and choose to go in the direction of joy and fulfillment."

Basically, you are becoming a new person – you became a mom and now you're a mom who is seeking a more meaningful career. Career changes are times of *big* transitions. They can be downright exhausting and taxing. And when there are tiny people clinging to your ankles demanding another bowl of Whole O's while you do it? That's a whole new level of exhaustion.

To make this career change, you've gotta take care of yo'self, momma! Seriously.

Ask for Help

I'm about to blow your mind: You are not Superwoman. You can't do it all. And, really, why would you want to? What do you get for trying to do all the things and be all the things for all the people? Burnout, that's what.

There's this idea in our culture that, as a mom, you are supposed to be a Superperson. Mother's Day cards, memes, articles, other people's expectations, your expectations – all support the incredibly damaging idea that, as a mom, you can do it all with no help from others.

We are supposed to work, clean our homes, wear whipped-cream bikinis to delight our partners, care for our kids, run all the errands, buy all the gifts, exercise, chauffeur, and love every second if it, with smiles on our face, no less. All by ourselves.

It's pure hogwash.

Can we please stand up together and loudly say, "I quit!"? "I quit this expectation for myself and for others." We can do a lot – oh boy, can we ever do a lot with our fierce momma strength, crazy cool gifts, and love for our families to fuel us. We get it all done! But we can't do it all and we can't do it alone.

Let's stop trying to.

* * *

I was asked once how we can show our kids how to receive kindness as well as give it. The answer is *showing* them how to receive it, by asking for help when we need it; by accepting help graciously when it's offered; by showing them that when they need help, they can ask for it, no matter what it's about.

You get support from your Soul as it gives you clues about what next to do. And then there's support from others. We're all trying to do too much and we're trying to do it alone.

Let's lean on each other instead. Okay? Because accepting help is a gift that we give the person who offers it.

Have you ever offered to help someone who you knew who could really use a break? Of course you have. We do it all the time. How often do people turn down help when you offer? I'm betting it's all the time. How does that make you feel? A little sad? It's not a big deal most of the time, but it does start to add up and affect the friendship. It really does. People *like* to feel needed and like you trust them to help you out. Truth.

How do we remedy this? *We ask for the help.* It may not be easy at first. It can feel weird – shameful almost – to admit that we are in need of help and let someone do it if you're not used to it. Sometimes it can feel downright horrible to admit weakness. But this feeling is like any other feeling and it can be questioned and felt without attaching to it. We can go deeper with it. Find out what's it's trying to tell us. And then let it go.

The more we do this, the easier it gets. That weird feeling starts to feel less weird and it's possible to look at the help with gratitude and see it as the act of love and service that it is. The more we do this, the more we take off of our plates and the more we get to feel love and gratitude. Sounds pretty good, right?

Emotional Support

You need fans to pull off this asking for help thing. One, at the minimum; more, if you've got them. You need people who are in your corner who can help you when you're feeling low, celebrate with you when you're winning at life, and brainstorm with you when you get stuck.

These fans can be partners, friends, mentors, coaches, or anyone else who looks at you and sees *you* and what you want to accomplish and can help you along the way to do the things you want to do.

Support looks different to each of us, but it must always feel like love to you and not like fake support wrapped up in competition, jealousy, or hostility. Your fan must be joyfully on your side and wish nothing but the best for you. Do you have that person as a partner or friend? Do you have more than one?

If not, the good news is this position can be filled by a life coach or mentor. You can also go looking for a pal to support you. Is there someone you've lost touch with who you can reconnect with? Are there meet-up groups you can join? Networking groups? Another great way to find support is online in Facebook groups.

The only requirement is that you are fully yourself and able to offer the same love and support you are seeking in return for the love and support you get from others. Be the support you need. Give the support you need. Receive openly the support you need.

* * *

Kira is a client of mine who decided to make the jump from her good-enough job as a home-based mortgage broker to following her dream of becoming a nutritionist. Midway through the schooling in her nutrition program, she was close to having a breakdown. She had piled school on top of her brokerage business work, parenting her son, doing all the housework, and working another part-time job, and so wasn't taking time for herself. She was drowning and thought that she had no one to help or to support her.

Kira had a bad case of Superwomanitis and desperately needed to ask for support. With her family far away, she turned to her husband who had never taken on much in the way of housework before. It was stupid hard for her to admit to him that she needed his help, but she eventually broke down and told him exactly how she felt – like she was drowning – and what she needed for support from him. Initially, he wasn't thrilled at the change to his own workload, but he did pitch in, because he loved being able to support Kira while she worked hard at her dream.

After working together to get to the end of Kira's school year, they ended up with a stronger marriage, because Kira had been able to admit and accept that she needed help. Chores got done. The pressure eased. And she found some breathing room in which to finish her courses with high marks. She no longer like she was going to crumple into a sobbing mess every second of the day.

We call that winning.

The Soul-Care Process

Self-care is one of the most important steps to this whole process – perhaps even the most important. You can't skip it or none of this is going to work. Soul-filled life-changing decisions don't come about when we ignore our own needs and allow exhaustion and burnout to rule. To do this, you genuinely have to care about your own well-being. You have to love yourself.

Now, that doesn't mean that you need to love everything about yourself all the time. What it does mean is that you need to love yourself more than you dislike yourself. You believe that your positives outweigh your negatives and you take the time to invest in your own care, wellness, and happiness, by making Soul Care a priority for you. You listen to your Soul and do what you need to, even if it's hard. Especially if it's hard.

This all goes deeper than a trip to the salon to tame the curls, spa days, solo time to run errands, and well-loved hobbies. Soul Care is about learning to listen to what you *really* need in a moment in order to feel the way you want to be feeling. It's about connecting to your body and your Soul and listening to their messages. It's about following the Soul crumbs and nudges. It's about telling the truth, living in integrity. and loving yourself when you're not perfect or when you think you've failed.

It's about returning home. Home is the place where your Soul replenishes, revives, and fills up. and where you feel whole, well, loved, and cherished. The way home for you may be simple or complex, require five minutes to get there, or require a year to get to.

It's completely worth the journey.

* * *

When do you practice Soul Care? Constantly. But, specifically, anytime you are feeling wistful, longing, bereft, angst-ridden, restless, out of sorts, pulled apart, or weary to your bones. The crappier and more stressed you feel, the more Soul Care you need. Make the time, take the time, to figure out what you need.

What does your need look like? Sometimes reading a familiar book or poem will give you the self-care you need. Sometimes going for a walk in nature will reconnect you with your Soul. Going for a haircut may do it, because, Lord knows how amazing it feels to come out looking like a million bucks after wearing spit-up and Cheerios-encrusted locks for days on end. Sometimes self-care will mean going for a soothing massage. It can be a long drive. It can be hiring a sitter so you can nap for three hours uninterrupted. It can be about booking a plane ticket to visit a friend. Or deciding that you're ready to have sex again and making a plan to seduce your partner.

Sometimes it's about giving up the body hatred and choosing to love your new-mom body instead.

Often, it's not what you think it should be. Soul Care is not always about pampering, indulgences, or napping. It might not take the form of the things that you would normally associate with "self-care." Sometimes it's about cleaning out a drawer or an entire closet so you feel a tiny bit of control over the chaos that reigns and feel some accomplishment. Or hiring someone to do it for you because you want to feel ease and spaciousness without taxing yourself. Sometimes it's forgiving someone. Or it can be having an overdue, difficult conversation with someone who has hurt you. Or it's crying in the tub with a bowl of ice cream and a glass of wine and letting yourself feel the sadness, hurt, frustration, or anger. It might be deciding to quit a hated job or firing your dog-walker.

Sometimes it's hugging your kids or dog. Sometimes it's feeling angry and going for a run or doing yoga even when you don't feel like it. Soul Care can be spending time cleaning up your online home by deleting friends off Facebook, deleting emails, unsubscribing to newsletters, or simplifying your apps. For you, Soul Care might look like seeking out new people to go for a coffee with. It might be ranting and releasing, or integrating a deep, hidden part of yourself. It might be booking that doctor appointment to get that rash looked at.

Sometimes Soul Care is about taking a leap and trying something new for a career.

It's not always sexy or indulgent. But if it's Soul Care, it's exactly what you need.

Though Soul Care can take many forms, the end result is that it makes you feel good – lighter, freer, happier, more joyful – even if it sometimes takes a bit of time for that result to appear (that's where learning to trust your Soul and Body Guide is so valuable).

At its heart, Soul Care is a prayer to your Soul, asking it what you need most. In fact, that's the exact question to ask: "What do I need most right now? What would feel the most like love?" And then going and doing that thing, while trusting that your Soul is guiding you with the highest vision for you in mind.

Soul-Care Exercise

This exercise is about taking the time to find your way to your Soul's home.

To begin, take three to five deep belly breaths. Shake off your to-do list. Shake off your day up until now. Breathe deeply again. Sink down into relaxation. Feel your whole body release tension. Feel your shoulders ease down and relax. Take another big, deep breath. And one more.

Now remember back to a time when you were having the best time; when you were doing something that made you happy; when you felt free, relaxed, full of joy; when time stopped; when your heart felt full; when you felt like you were home.

Break that memory down into the simplest elements by asking yourself:

- What was I doing?
- Where was I?"
- Who was I with?"
- What do I see?
- What do I hear? What other sounds remind me of that time?
- What do I smell? What other smells take me back to that experience?
- What do I taste?
- What do I feel on my skin? On my fingertips?

- How do I feel? What emotions do I feel? Where in My body do I feel them?

Take all the elements from the answers you gave and come up with a name for them as a whole. You can call it something like *Bob* or *Summer Story* or *Peace & Calm*. When you desperately need to return back to your Soul home, ask yourself, "What can I do in the time I have to feel like (insert your name for your Soul home place)?"

Maybe eating some strawberries will take you back to feeling that way. Maybe it's walking around among some trees. Maybe it's lighting a candle that smells like it did in your story. Maybe it's calling someone who shares that memory. Maybe it's doing that very same thing again. Whether you have five minutes or a month, you can return home and care for your Soul. In return, you'll have renewed energy to tackle this next big life adventure of a career change.

Take some time now to create a list that you can refer to of things you can do within certain time frames to head yourself toward your Soul home place. Start by writing down the following time spans:

- 5 minutes
- 30 minutes
- 1 hour
- 2-4 hours
- 1 day
- 3+ days

Spend fifteen to twenty minutes filling in as many things as you can think of that you can do in those amounts of time that take you home and make you feel amazing and satisfied right down to the Soul.

* * *

So often, we do the same things over and over again for self-care. They become habits and we forget about the things that we truly love to do. Now you have a list that you can go back to when your usual things aren't working so well. This is invaluable! Don't skip this exercise. You'll be surprised at how much it helps to have your list.

Soul-Care Basics

The magic and mystery of Soul aside, there are a few simple, basic ways to take care of yourself that are often glossed over or forgotten in the rush of life with small kids.

Sleep

Get more of it. Get a lot of it. Get as much as you can. Think of sleep as the cure-all for everything. Feeling under the weather? Get some sleep. Brain going off the deep end thinking that you're crazy for changing careers? Sleep! Kids keeping you up at night? Go for a nap. Have an hour of alone time but can't think of a single enjoyable thing you want to be doing? Sleep. Feeling like everything is awful and impossible and you're never going to do anything other than feel this way? Sleep is the cure. Everything will feel *much* better once you've rested *and* as an added bonus, you'll get more done in the long run. Trust me.

Catnaps. Fifteen-minute naps. Full hour-long naps. Naps with your head on your arms at your desk. Long nights of sleep. Naps while your kids are napping. Quick naps while your kids watch some Elmo. Trading nap time with your partner. Interrupted naps. Good naps. Not so good naps. All of it helps.

Water

Drink enough to be fully hydrated, no matter how annoying it is to pee with little kids who can't or won't leave you alone to do so.

Food

Eat healthy food that makes you feel good. I'm not telling you that you need to stress over food choices or go on a diet. I mean that there is food that you can eat that makes your body feel good and makes you full of energy... and there's food that does not do that. Choose the good-feeling stuff. Use your Body Guide to tell what you need to eat. The Body Guide works amazingly well at helping us figure out what we need to eat.

Exercise

Move your body in ways that feel amazing to you. Hate yoga but love to do interpretive dance to Michael Bolton's collection of 90s pop ballads? Dance your gorgeous little heart out. (Because he really does want to know how he can live without you, now that you are gone.)

Feeling overwhelmed, even though you've gotten enough sleep? Go for a walk outside in nature. Bonus points if you can do it solo.

Self-Compassion

Many of us have an easy enough time finding compassion and kindness for others but have a hard time extending the same to ourselves. We go through our days with a very mean voice in our heads that constantly beats us up for all the little and big mistakes we make. You know the one. If we talking to our friends and family the way we've learned to talk to ourselves, no one would want to be around us. Fact.

Learning to speak to yourself nicely, leaning to befriend yourself, and learning to lead with love and kindness plays a big part in freeing your Soul. One way to do this is to catch those mean thoughts we have toward ourselves and, instead of believing them, offer ourselves some kindness and love instead. Banishing the inner mean girl is a perk of this whole process

After I introduced this concept to a client of mine in a session, she told me that until I mentioned the idea of her inner mean girl, she had never even noticed just how mean she was to herself. We often don't even realize how mean our inner voices are. It's *that* ingrained in us to think mean things and judge ourselves.

How do we do we beat this? Start by noticing what you are saying to yourself when you make a mistake or when something goes wrong. Ask yourself if what you just thought about yourself is a kind and compassionate thought, or if it's your inner mean girl coming out. It's your mean inner girl when she says things that you would never in a million years say to someone else. Once you've noticed and stopped the mean thought in its tracks, gently repeat this affirmation: "May I be happy, may I be healthy, may I be safe, and may I live with ease."

Repeat as needed throughout the day.

CHAPTER 4

Find Your Gifts

*"I've come to believe that each of us has
a personal calling that's as unique as a
fingerprint – and that the best way to succeed
is to discover what you love and then find a
way to offer it to others in the form of service,
working hard, and also allowing the energy
of the universe to lead you."*
– Oprah Winfrey

The second you became a mom you became a new person. It may have happened when the strip turned blue or when you first held that scrunchy-faced bundle in your arms. Or it may have happened later and differently, depending how your child came to be your child.

But it happened.

Old You vs. New You

You are no longer the same person you were.

Which means that there's some work to do to let go of the old you so you can embrace the new you. We do this by taking some time to mourn. Whether you need five minutes to do this or a few weeks, let it happen. There is beauty in mourning the old so that you can accept what is in front of you now.

Mourn the person that you used to be. Mourn the person you thought you would be. Think of the person you thought you would be at the age that you are now. Did you think your life would be different than it is? Did you think you'd have a different partner? Different children? A different body? A different home? Think of all the things you thought your life would be like.

Now think of the person that you were before having kids. Think of what you did with your time. Think of what you looked like. Think of your priorities and who you used to spend time with. Think of all the places you went and the work you did. Think of how it was with your partners, friends, and family.

Think of it all and then notice the differences between what you thought it would be like and what it was like to be the old you.

Emotions might come up here, so practice feeling and releasing them. All emotions are valid here in this process – anger, sadness, happiness, joy – any of those, and any feelings you have, are messengers sending you information. Think of all you have lost and all you have gained in your journey from non-parent to parent. Think of how far you have come in many ways.

Feel what needs to be felt as you mourn and release what you thought your life would be like and what it has been for you. Breathe into it. Feel it. Release it with love and gratitude.

Begin to think about where you are now as a mom. All that you have gained. Everything you have lost. Everything that you want for yourself right now and everything you want in the future.

Lean into it and begin accepting where you are right now. Breathe here for a while.

Begin to look for the love and gratitude for this place you are in. Right now. Stay here for a while. Stay here in the love and gratitude for it all. Breathe.

You might find that you need to do this a few times to really mourn and to be able to let go of the old you. It takes as long as it takes. There might be many layers or there might not be a lot to explore here. There is no wrong answer.

Your Genius

You have many gifts. Many wonderful gifts that, when you use them in service of others, can light you up so much that you shine so bright it looks like you have light beams coming out of you. You have a calling, right from your Soul self, to use your gifts. It doesn't matter what label you call yourself – lawyer, hairdresser, psychiatrist, welder – when you use the gifts that make you uniquely *you* in a way that lights you up – the things you have a passion for it – and that helps others in some way, it fulfills you like no other work can. Answering the call to do this kind of work is an answer to your Soul's Calling.

We need people in this world who use their gifts, genius, and talents. I honestly believe that if we do the work to really see ourselves and we figure out what our gifts are and then get brave enough to use them, we heal ourselves in many ways and, in turn, inspire others to find and use theirs, thus creating more and more people who are doing what they are here to do. Beautiful stuff.

The more you can see yourself and your gifts, the more you can confidently start moving toward using them and finding amazing work that you love to do.

It took me a long time to be able to see myself and my gifts. I'd never really known that I had gifts. I hadn't realized that knowing what they were would make finding meaningful work so much easier. That had never occurred to me. Maybe it's never really occurred to you to go digging for this either. It seems we're often pointed toward work that we like or toward elusive passions, but don't really look at the whole of ourselves and our preferences in order to paint a picture of a life and career we would love down to our Soul.

I wasn't really able to do this until I went off on a retreat in Mexico to explore this issue. In my line of work as a life coach, I have to have a strong sense of self (you know, so I can guide people toward theirs). Before that trip to Mexico, I really had no idea who I or and how I could do that.

After four days with some amazing women, I finally had the pieces I needed to put it all together. I could see that my gifts of being grounded, funny (often out of nowhere), and clever could help my clients feel at ease. My abilities to see people for who they are and have them feel accepted, along with my trustworthiness are all incredible assets in the line of work I am called to do. I have an ability to both be edgy and soft, fierce and vulnerable. I have a soft heart, fierce strength, and can be a great leader. I can often see the whole of a problem and the challenges it brings, but, at the same time, I can also see the tiny steps needed to move forward and solve the problem. I can feel other people's emotions and deftly read the subtext of things going on in a room. I have a finely tuned hogwash detector and am not afraid to use it.

The ways I choose to use these gifts and the support I need to build my business are tempered by what I love to do, my preferences, and who I am at my core. I love to read and write, so I am writing this knowledge and encouragement for you as a book instead of doing a video series. I am an introvert, so I will do work with individuals and small groups rather than do large-audience speaking gigs. I love to work with Excel and have a love of stationery, so I will do my own business finances tracking and shop for my own office supplies, but I don't like cooking or cleaning, so I will buy healthy pre-made meals and make use of a cleaning service.

I start things quickly and tend to follow through on them if they are important to me, but I do have a tendency to take on too much and so I know I need more support in this area.

I tell you all that to show you that knowing my gifts and the way I do things positions me really well to succeed in my business. With this information about myself, I can look at my strengths and weaknesses and know how and where to fill in the gaps. I know what I am good at doing, and I know where I don't shine – so I can hire that stuff out.

Knowing yourself and how you do things is valuable information when looking at a new career.

Your Gifts

It's time for you to list your gifts.

Take 15 minutes and write out all of the gifts that you have. This can feel daunting when you're not sure about your gifts, but simple, little things are great clues. Think of them as your Soul's calling puzzle pieces. The more pieces you can collect, the bigger and clearer the picture on the puzzle – your gifts – becomes. No one needs to see this list but you, so go ahead and write down anything you think of that could be clues to gifts. You can write things like:

- "I can pee standing up."
- "I can sing karaoke like no one else."
- "I can shower and get dressed in two minutes."

There is nothing too small or too big to add to your list.

What are you trained in? Make a list of skills, education, and training that you already have. What have you learned? Write it all down. Anything and everything you can think of. It doesn't have to be a big list. You can have two items on it and still figure all of this out. Or it can be a small book. Again, there's no wrong answer here.

Asking Those Who Love You

If you're having a hard time seeing yourself, or even if you're not, you can ask people that you know for help in uncovering your gifts. Sometimes it's useful for us to see how others see us. You can email them or call them. Here's a sample script to get you started:

"Hi, {insert pal's name}

I would love and appreciate it if you could help me out. I'm uncovering my gifts and what makes me unique and I would like your honest answers to the these few questions:

- When you think of me, what qualities come to mind?
- What do you see as my particular gifts? What are some of my talents?
- What makes me different and unique?
- What do I do really well?

Thank you!"

Change it up if you'd like, but make sure you generally ask the three main questions. Collect the answers and mine them for clues to your gifts and talents.

* * *

The next question to ask yourself is what are you ridiculously good at? What do people compliment you on all the time? What do you do so well that it doesn't even feel like it's special? This can be anything from making the world's best cup of coffee to having incredible planning and research abilities. Do you connect people without even thinking about it? Do you dance really well? Do you love making videos? Do you make people laugh?

Make a list in your journal and then answer the following questions.

- What do you spend your time doing?
- What are you doing when you lose track of time? (This may be a few different things.)
- Who do you wish you could trade lives with? Why?
- What do you want that you don't have? Why?
- What do people ask for your help with?
- What feels easy for you?
- What do you want to be doing more of?
- Who do you love spending time with? Why?
- What can't you not do? Or what can't you not learn about?

Using the answers to those questions, see if patterns start to emerge. Often, when the puzzle pieces start to come together, they reveal an answer so obvious it makes you blush that you didn't see it sooner. As in, the answers have been in plain sight this whole time.

Much like Ellie wasn't able to see and accept her own intuition, a friend I was chatting with the other day was very much unable to see her own gifts, the passion and Soul-calling that was right in front of her face.

We were at dinner and Lucy was describing how hard it had been since she and her husband lost their jobs in marketing. While at her previous job, she'd started taking courses to become a personal trainer and had fallen in love with it. She had also spent a lot of time taking fitness courses.

I'd known about Lucy's love of fitness for a while, so it wasn't shocking to me that she kept taking courses and learning new things. What *was* shocking to me was that she was considering going to school to become a daycare assistant. I asked her why and she mumbled some answer about it being convenient for her and her kids, since she could take them to work with her and didn't have the money to pay childcare costs. Now, that is a great perk to the job if you actually want to be a daycare assistance.

But, clearly, Lucy did not. She is in love with fitness. I mentioned to her that she could offer a subscription video series and teach fitness classes online. Her response was that she couldn't be a fitness person like that because she likes to drink beer too much. She wanted to be a fitness person who enjoyed life and didn't count every calorie. I told her that that was part of her charm and one of her gifts – that she was very real. Lots of people crave that.

To further compound my point, our waitress had overheard and said how much she would love to follow a beer-drinking, healthy, fitness-loving person who taught students to enjoy the good things in life, because a beer belly didn't mean a person wasn't fit. Thinking that Lucy would see her gift for sure then, after such incredible synchronistic evidence, she just shook her head again and said she couldn't do it.

She couldn't see a path forward for herself because she wasn't listening. Not really. The Soul nudge was ignored.

What Soul nudges might you be ignoring? What do you do so well that people always ask you for help with it? What comes so easy to you that you can't help do it and get frustrated that other people can't? Again, there are no wrong answers here. Anything can be a clue.

Transitions

How you do one thing is how you do everything. If you take a look back at one (or a few) times you went through a big transition, you can get a picture of how you generally move through challenges. When you know this, you can recognize patterns of where you tend to get stuck, what you tend to feel during a big transition, and what you do to get yourself out.

1. Pick a big change you've gone through – the kind of a change where there was a Before and an After and you were really different afterward.
2. What ended for you because of that transition? What changed? What kinds of losses did you experience? An example: By becoming a mom, I lost the freedom to go anywhere and do anything anytime I wanted to. I lost the ability to sleep when I wanted to. I lost the young, carefree me.
3. What did you gain?
4. What are some of the emotions you felt during that change? Try to pick out the ones that repeated often.

5. What did you focus on the most during that change?
6. You made it through the transition. What helped you? What did you do to get through it? Were there strategies that you used? Who or what did you lean on?

Review your answers. Do you see more now about how you make it through it? Do you see the unique parts of yourself that helped you through? If not, pick another one or two times of transition and answer the questions above for those, until you start to see at least a bit of a pattern emerge.

Add your findings to your list of puzzle pieces.

Your Shadow

Your shadow is where you put things that you aren't comfortable sharing with others. They're the things that make you cringe a little – or a lot – when you think of them. I talked a bit about your shadow in previous chapters. Let's dig a little deeper now.

In your journal, write you answers to the following questions:

- What did you used to do but don't do any longer, for fear of a negative reaction?
- What did you used to do for fun but don't anymore?
- What do you want to do more of but won't allow yourself?

I used to push so much into my shadow that it was heavy to cart around. One of the biggest parts of me that I put in there was my leadership abilities. In grade two, I used to boss around everyone. I had a whole group of people I was the "leader" of. I was probably being a jerk in some ways – I can't really remember. What I do remember is my mom coming back from a parent-teacher interview and telling me that I was considered a "ringleader."

I didn't know what that was exactly, but the way mom explained it to me made me believe that, whatever it was, it was a bad thing and I probably should stop being one. So I took the part of me that wanted to lead others and shoved it right down into my shadow and decided that, from then on, I would do my best to follow, not lead. I spent the next 25 or so years hiding behind other people who wanted to lead, being their "second." I let them shine. Or so I thought. Leading was and is a big part of who I am, and it would come out at times, making me inconsistent and awkward.

I took that part of myself out of my shadow recently and can't help but wonder what would have happened if I'd not hid that part of myself away in the first place. If I'd found a way to lead and let that part of myself grow and be nurtured, I would probably be queen of something by now.

* * *

There are many other fun assessments one can do to discover more about oneself. I often have my clients do them so we can help identify what they're good at and where their strengths lie.

I had my client Diane take the Kolbe test so we could see how she worked best. It turned out she was assessed as a high Quick Start, but not so high on Follow Thru, which is why she was fantastic at starting projects in her business but terrible at finishing them. She often beat herself up for not being able to finish what she'd started, and we spent a few sessions talking about strategies she could use to get stuff done.

As an INFJ on the Meyers-Briggs, I was finding it hard to get out there and network in large rooms full of people. I would clam up and not be able to talk to people, defeating the point in going. Although I had a high 'I' (introvert) in the assessment, I was trying to do things that 'E's (extroverts) enjoy more, and then beating myself up for it when, really, I do so much better in smaller groups in quieter spaces where I can hear myself think. Changing how I expect myself to go out and conquer the marketing world shifted a lot for me and made marketing easier.

Knowing my results of various assessments ended up pulling together more pieces of the puzzle and I could clearly see where I could grow as a person and as a coach – while honouring the parts of me that I can't change.

CHAPTER 5

Divine Discontent

"Discontent is the first necessity of progress."
–Thomas Edison.

I know that you want a change in your career, or you wouldn't have picked up this book. Something about it isn't right. Do you know what?

Make Your List

Let's start putting together the pieces of what you *do* want by, first, talking about what you don't want. This is where we get to complain about all the less than awesome things that we didn't like. Fun!

When I was working at an office job, before I had kids, I would sit there and think about what life would be like for me if I did have kids and still worked there. I thought about the long days and then going back home to cook dinner for the kids and then doing bedtime and then finally getting time to relax. It didn't seem impossible to do, or that anything was really wrong with it, but it also didn't seem like anything I really wanted for myself as a future mom. Thinking of that scenario is a big reason why I pushed myself to find something else.

That something else was wrong for me, as I've discussed, but that's beside the point for what I want to talk about now. I knew that full-time office work wasn't going to be a fit for me when I became a mom.

I'd already started my list of Divine Discontent.

Soon, others things joined the list. I didn't like being at work doing nothing – if I was going to be doing work I didn't much care for, I wanted to be busy the whole day. Sitting there and doing nothing but not being able to leave was torture for me. I didn't want to only live for the weekends. I didn't want to be limited to three weeks of vacation a year. I didn't like working in the morning. And so on. My list of Divine Discontent grew.

Your turn. What do you want to change about your work? What don't you like about your work life now? What makes it onto your Divine Discontent list of things that you no longer want now that you're a momma?

Set a timer for 15 minutes, take a few deep breaths and let yourself go. Turn it into a really great Lettin' It Go: I Hate My Job list. Go as whiny as you want. Let loose. Swear. Don't worry about being nice. Let it *all* out. Write it down.

Don't skip doing this. You're going to use your answers later to make things better.

Let Go

For the longest time, I believed that I had to continue working as a massage therapist. I had a lot of reasons: I'd spent a lot of money on the course; it was a perfectly fine career; I liked it well enough; I had everything I needed for it; it was easy to find a job; it paid decently. And on and on. I spent so much time trying to think my way into liking it that I forgot to really look at what I didn't like about it.

I didn't like the way it made me feel afterward. I didn't like having a boss. I didn't like the expectation that I would work whenever a client asked. I didn't like the unreliable income. I didn't like building my business.

I tried so hard to convince myself that it was a good job for me that I only focused on the positives and I wouldn't let myself go to the negatives. Doing that landed me right back into Depressionland. Which confused me to no end. After all, massage was a pretty okay job, wasn't it? It was in the helping field, after all. It turned out that I needed to let it go in order to make way for the next thing in my life.

What are you holding onto that you need to let go of? Is it your career? Is it where you live? A relationship?

Great Expectations

Sometimes it's not the job that's the problem, but our expectations.

Have you spent a lot of time thinking about changing jobs, but nothing else appeals to you? Are you looking for your job to fulfill an empty part of you? Do you keep searching for the elusive, magic career that will make everything better, make you rich, and remove your problems?

If so, you're looking in the wrong place. You're looking for something outside yourself to make you happy. In truth, there isn't a single job out there that can make you happy and fulfill you if you're not willing to do the work to make yourself happy and fulfill yourself *first*.

Happiness is, first and foremost, an inside job. Careers and jobs can add to that happiness and fulfillment, by using your gifts and helping you be of service in a way that brings joy and satisfaction, but there is nothing out there that can do that on its own.

Thinking otherwise is like thinking that you'll be happy once you lose weight or have another baby or find the perfect partner. It doesn't ever work that way.

Before continuing on this Soul journey, ask yourself if you're looking for a job to fill something that can't be filled by work.

* * *

One of the things I hear a lot as a mom, and that I believe with my whole heart, is that the path to peace as a mom is to lower our expectations. And then lower them some more. Whether our expectation is about the cleanliness of the house, how our kids spend their time (fewer activities might be a great thing), or the way our partners show up for us, lowered expectations can only bring happiness and peace. Really. As contrary as it sounds, it's true.

What do I mean by this? Changing the expectation that anything outside of ourselves can makes us happy lowers stress and brings more freedom to enjoy life as it is.

This doesn't mean that we can't enjoy a clean home or have to live in squalor. Or that we have to tolerate rude, unkind, or belligerent behavior. Or that we have to stay in jobs and careers that aren't right for us. It means that we're not superwomen who can do, be, and have it all. We have to be realistic with our time and our energy. Sometimes, being realistic means lowering our expectations and taking off the perfectionist hat in order to be happier and have more satisfaction. It takes the pressure off so we can breathe. From there, we can assess what we actually want and need.

The Real Problem

Is the problem you *think* you have the actual problem you have?

In one of my sessions with Maisie, she mentioned that she didn't have a clear space to work. There was too much clutter in her home and she didn't have an office to work in. The mess distracted her and she found it hard to work on her business. She really wanted her husband to finish their basement so she could work there, but he wasn't willing to do it for her.

Digging deeper, we discovered that what she was really upset about was her husband being in her space, since he worked from home as well; her kids not helping her out; and feeling like everything was on her shoulders to do and fix. She had Superwomanitis in a big way and needed help seeing that she really wanted was help with setting boundaries and delegating.

Within a couple of sessions, she had recruited her kids to help out more, had found a creative way to get her own space so she could work, and recognized that she couldn't do it all herself and that what had been getting in the way of her work wasn't the clutter, but her inability to set clear boundaries for her family and ask for help.

* * *

Is there something holding you back in a similar way that you need to dig deeper into? Very often, the problem we think we have isn't our real problem. We need to did deeper to figure out what is really going on.

What's really going on with your career unrest? Do you want a new job? Or do you want your current position to be more accommodating? Do you need to change to a different company? Move to a different position within the same company?

If you are ready for a new career adventure, wonderful! We can get you there. If not, if you need some rearranging of your current job, we can do that, too. But it's important that you're clear on what it is that you don't want, don't like, and won't put up with anymore – and why. From that place, it's possible to move forward into what you do want.

It's kinda like you've gone on a trip through a transition and are now pausing to look through your luggage to make sure that what you're bringing along for the next ride are all the things that you really want to have with you.

Anger as Fuel

You can mine your anger for more clues.

A different way to look for lovely, meaningful work is to dig into what pisses you off. What do you want to change in the world? What do you want to change in your city? What breaks your heart and demands that you take action? What do you want to change in your current career? Write that down.

What gets me fired up is when gorgeous, talented women I know sell themselves short and settle for things that aren't good enough for them; when women choose to hide rather than shine; when people avoid their feelings or avoid hard things because they think that's easier; when people decide that being who they truly are is okay for other people to do, but not for them.

All of those things have led me to this path, to writing this book, to my desire to help people shine as brightly as they can. Like Supa Stars!

CHAPTER 6

Dream That Dream

"Dreams are whispers from your Soul."
–Unknown

You've met your beautiful Soul, connected to your Body Guide, and know exactly what you don't want. Now comes the part where you get to dream, darling. We get so wrapped in our heads, in the day-to-day living, that we often forget to let ourselves dream. We think that because something is one way right now that it can't change. We get so caught up in the minute details of caring for our kids and households and partners that we miss the moments to let our imaginations soar over the possibilities. We dismiss our longings as frivolous and say, "Not right now," and go back to folding the tiny laundry. Our dreams seem too big for this time in our lives so we quiet them down to wait for an easier time.

We forget our power. This means we let our current level of tiredness dictate what we will be doing later.

I'll tell you right now that there is no easier time than now. And nothing is impossible. Everything is figureoutable. You can do anything. Not everything – but you can do anything!

Career Daydreams

Indulge in some career daydreaming right now. What would you want to do? Where would you want to do it? How would it feel?

Now spend some time remembering the dreams that you had when you were growing up.

- When you were five, what did you want to be when you grew up?
- How about at eight? Did it change?
- At fourteen?
- What sorts of things did you really, really want to be?

Write down in your journal everything that comes to mind.

Let's focus more specifically on when you were between the ages of five and eight specifically. Close your eyes, breathe deeply, and go back to that time. Do you remember what you wanted to be when you were that age? It might have been anything. I mean it when I say it might have been anything. A client of mine, Michelle, wanted to be a garbage truck when she was around that age.

Take those things you have written down and look deeper by answering the following questions:

1. Why did you want to be that?
2. What about it was most exciting to you?
3. How did you feel when you thought about doing that work?

Michelle wanted to be a garbage truck because she liked the idea of slowly driving around and saying hi to everyone while making things prettier. She was excited by the freedom of being able to go anywhere. She felt free and happy when she thought about what being a garbage truck would mean for her.

When I was seven or so, I wanted to be a writer. I had an old school desk that my mom had bought for me and I kept my notebook in it with a list of all the chapters I was going to write. I wanted to be a writer so that I could tell stories to people. That was exciting to me because I loved putting words onto paper and seeing the magic of them coming together to tell a story. I loved reading and it was exciting that I could create something I loved. I felt content, satisfied, free, smart, and accomplished when I thought about being a writer.

Michelle really wants a job where she has the freedom to go to lots of different places, at her own pace, with lots of people around to chat with, and she values feeling free and happy in her work.

I want a job where I can talk to people through words and see some magic come from it. I value feeling content, important, smart, and accomplished in the work that I do. Those are all things that I still want and value in my work. I still want to be a writer and see magic while feeling that way. My seven year old self knew it all along, even if I forgot along the way.

Michelle, on the other hand, most definitely no longer wants to be a garbage truck. But the things that old wish told her are still true for her in her visual design business for retail stores: she loves the happiness of talking to lots of people and while being free to choose her projects and schedule. She loves making things more beautiful.

You can do this process with any job you've ever wanted to have – no matter what age you were when you wanted it – and dig deeper into the Soul puzzle pieces to tease out the crux of what you want. You can never have too many of those old career or job wishes, because they all add up to giving you a more clear picture of your Soul's desires in the end.

Keep on dreaming on!

Ideal Week

How do you want to spend your time each week?

Sit back, put up your feet, and get ready to dream up your version of your ideal week. You're going to get super specific – from the clothes that hang in your closet to the sounds you hear, and the time you go to bed.

Sitting comfortably, with your journal and a pen handy, take some deep breathes. Clear away your day up until now from your mind. Relax everything in your body that's holding tension. Keep breathing.

Start by picking you least favourite day of the week. Start when you first wake up and open your eyes. Look around you at where you wake up. What time is it? What's different? Where are you? What are you wearing? What city are you in? Get up and do your new morning routine. Get dressed in your closet full of clothes you love. Note what the clothes are. What do you do next? What and when do you eat? Who is around you? Do you go out to work? What do you do for a living? How do you fill your time? When does your work day end? What do you do afterward? What do you do last before bed? What time do you go to bed? What smells are around you as you wind down from your day? What sights? What do you hear?

Go through each day of your week. Dream lovely things. Make it your ideal week in every way. Write it down.

When you're done, go through it and pick out the parts that really make your heart jump with excitement. Ask yourself:

1. What's different between my life now and my ideal week?
2. What do I absolutely love and adore from my ideal week that needs to happen in my life now?
3. What clues can I get from everything that is different from my ideal week and my life now?

Make a list of everything you've discovered – all the puzzle pieces. Are you noticing a theme yet?

Flipping It Around

Now let's go look back at the work you did with your Lettin' It Go: I Hate My Job list from Chapter 5 – everything you hated from your previous job. Look at each thing you wrote down and flip it to the opposite to identify exactly what you do want.

Here's an example. If you wrote "I hate loud co-workers who talk about boring inane things," you might flip it to "I want to work for myself and have clients who talk of nothing but Soulful amazing things."

Something like "I hate being disrespected and overworked" could turn into "I love being valued and having just the right amount to do."

"I hate smelly microwaved lunch smells" could turn into "I want to eat delicious, fresh lunches at home with my kids each day."

Get creative. Flip your Lettin' It Go list items to things that make you giddy with joy when you read them. You might have work with a few of them to really find the opposite that makes your Soul-self quiver with delight. It's worth it.

Your Current Job

Let's talk about the elephant in the room. The elephant that you're trying to avoid by buying and reading this book. Your current J. O. B.

It's true that there are things you dislike about it. There are things you no longer want to do, now that you have kids in the picture. But there are also things you love about your current job. Or did love. Or thought were pretty okay at one time. Right? If I'm wrong, skip this section. Lord knows, I've worked at enough Get Me Out of Here Now Jobs to know that sometimes they really do just suck, and there's nothing redeeming about them, and you really just wanna to pull the super-dramatic, "Well, I *quit* you jerk-noses!" before twirling and walking out the door, never to see or hear from those people again. If that's you, then skip this section and focus on the rest of the book.

For everyone else, let's talk about what is good enough about what you do right now – or what you most recently did.

1. What do you love about what you do/did?
2. What will you miss?
3. What drew you to that career in the first place?

I'll even ask the question the hard question: Are you sure you want to change careers? Sure, it's likely changed a lot for you since having a baby (or three), but are you really ready to leave?

When you read that question, what happens to your Body Guide readings? Do you hear any quiet voices whispering – or shouting – any message to you? Do you feel horrified at the idea of staying in your current role? Do you feel ready to tackle a new challenge, even if you're not quite sure what it tis? Notice what's happening to your body.

It's possible that what you want isn't more or different than what you have now, but only simpler. Maybe the Soul voice that's asking you for change isn't asking for you to change the career you have now, it's asking you to do less.

Maybe that involves selling your large home in the suburbs and moving to a townhouse in a quiet city neighborhood or to a smaller home in a town further away. Maybe it's buying some land and working from home while you care for your children, six dogs, four cats, three goats, and a dozen chickens. Maybe it's going part-time at your current job and learning to become Queen of Budgeting. Maybe it's deciding to become a stay-at-home mom.

Or maybe it is *more*. Maybe it's letting go of the idea of being a stay-at-home mom doing school pickups in leggings while holding a delicious hot coffee and talking to other moms about the antics of your kids. Maybe it is, instead, embracing that what you really do want is a Big Career. Maybe you want the empire. Maybe you want the high-rise condo downtown in a big city with a nanny to care for your kids and trips to all kinds of places with your family. Maybe you want to get the promotions and break the glass ceiling and take over like a ladyboss.

There is no wrong answer. There is only *your* answer.

* * *

Sometimes, as we've discussed, the problem isn't really your job. Sometimes it's feeling like you're going to miss out as a mom if you work longer hours than you'd like. Sometimes it's fear that you need to do more or be more or have more than you do, are, and have. Sometimes your career is good enough for you just as it is, but you need a tweak or two. Maybe a hard conversation needs to happen with your partner or boss.

A person – *you*, specifically – doesn't always need to be striving for more all the time. There's a magic that can happen within boredom and staying still. You can give yourself permission to rest where you are for a while, if that's absolutely the right thing for you and your family. *Or* you can give yourself permission to Really Go. For. It.

Connecting to your Soul may have given you this answer already. If moving on is going to be your new normal, let's continue on with dreaming and scheming!

Last, But Not Least – Money

How much money to do want to make? For real. It's important for you to know your numbers. I don't mean in a "How do I afford a career change?" kind of way. I mean in a "How much money do I want to make in my new career?" kind of way.

You need to know what your baseline income needs to be: what you need to bring home each month for necessities and bills. What's the minimum you need to make each month. Figure that out and you have your baseline income.

Now... dream bigger. What extras do you want each month? What do you want to be able to do with your family? Travel? Camp in a van down by the river for an entire season? Eat at fine dining places more often than not? Live on mac and cheese and make enough to pay for swimming lessons?

Again, and always, there are no wrong answers here. You can choose how you want to feel in your life and you can choose what are valid and completely awesome ways for you to live. You don't need to look at what anyone else has or wants. Or even what anyone else wants for you. Maybe you don't care how much you earn, as long as you have enough to pay for your bowling league fees each month. Maybe you want your own private plane. No judgement. Want what you want. Own it.

* * *

Money is nothing more than energy. You receive money in exchange for work that you do. You might not care much about money and yet have oodles of it. You might want more money very badly but are never quite able to make that happen. This book isn't about getting over money blocks or manifesting stacks of cold, hard cash. But I do want you to be able to look at how much your family needs to live, what you want to be able to do as a family, and what you want to be able to save for (like for when you're old and don't wanna work anymore).

When you know what your baseline income is, figure out what amount of money you want to earn that's above that. Use your Body Guide for this. The number you come up with shouldn't feel impossible and make you want to panic and cry, but it should feel a little unattainable, exciting, and slightly dangerous.

These can be rough numbers at this point, and there's no need to hold fast to them, but having a good sense of these numbers and dreaming about what you want your new income to look like starts to make it all that much more real and possible.

* * *

When I helped Maisie do this exercise, I asked her what she wanted to do with her family that she wasn't able to do now with her current income. Her answer – and this was right from the Soul – was that she wanted to travel with them. She wanted to be the one who made enough money for her family so that they could go to all sorts of amazing places together. She also wanted to go on retreats by herself, to recharge without her family around. As she talked about that, her body language and her voice changed. She came alive. I could see the moment when she finally figured out that she could make those things happen for herself and her family if she worked in her business a little bit differently. Magic.

That is the kind of reaction you are looking for as you do this exercise. With this and the other exercises in this book, look to let your Soul self come through and guide you, so you can see and feel your dreams at a deeper level. The aim is to feel like you're coming alive thinking about what you want to create for yourself and your family.

* * *

Ellie had already done the first part of the dreaming equation. She was in the process of setting up her dream massage therapy business at home so she could be with her family more. But it was really hard for her. She was working way too many hours and trying to fit in everyone who called and asked for a massage. She was bordering on burning out and not loving her work.

We hopped on a call and worked through her ideal week. As we went through it, Ellie figured out, for each day of her ideal week, how many massages she wanted to do and at what times of day. She also added in a ton of self-care time, time with her family, and time to just enjoy life. When she counted up the number of massages in her ideal week, she realized that it was the *exact* number that her family needed her to do to bring home enough money to live the good life they wanted.

She took a good look at where the gaps were between what she was already doing with her time and what she wanted to be doing with her time. She did some adjusting and tweaking and ended up adding in more time with friends and time for herself.

CHAPTER 7

Declare It!

"Where your talents and the needs of the
world cross; there lies your vocation."
−Aristotle

The world needs you to use your gifts. It's cheesy and yet, very true. The world needs happy, engaged people who are masters of their craft. The world needs professionals who are living from their Soul. It needs gorgeous goddesses of love who refuse to settle. It needs *you* to know, honour, and love your gifts and put them to good use being of service in ways that light you up like the shiny star that you are.

You were born with amazing talents and gifts. You may have discovered some of them by reading this book and doing the exercises. But, very often, it's not enough to know that piece of the puzzle and be able to come up with the dreamiest job you could ever imagine. What also comes into play are what you like to do, what you don't like to do, and your Soul

I might be the world's best swimmer (which I am definitely not), but if I hate water on my face (which I do), I most likely won't choose to go for a gold at the Olympics anytime soon (which I haven't). You might have a natural talent for cooking or baking, but not like to do it more than once a year. You might be the most organized person in the world in your own home, but would want to scream if you tried to run a home-organization business.

You have to *like* using your gifts. You have to *like* dealing with the less-than-ideal aspects that come with the job – or at least be able to tolerate them.

Take a look at your gifts, talents, skills that you have complied in your shiny little journal. Set a timer and sit down for 15 minutes and write down every single real or made-up job that you can think of that would pay you any amount. Everything you can think of. Everything you are qualified to do and everything you are not qualified to do. *Everything.*

Go further, into aspects of jobs: Do you want to own your own business? Do you want to be an employee? Do you want to do something in the middle – a contract freelance worker?

Now go back to Chapter 2 and do the Free Your Soul meditation again. Look at your list from a place of Soul and use your Body Guide to really feel into each of the things you wrote down on your jobs list. Don't *think* about it – *feel* it.

For each job, note what type of reaction your body had:

1. Nope!
2. Possible
3. Yesssss!

Declare It!

Take another look at the Possibles and the Yesssssses. What sticks out to you about them? Is there a theme? Did you identify a job/career that knocks your socks off and that you can't wait to get going on? Have you known it for a long time? Did the seven-year-old version of you know? Do you have a general idea about a job for you, based on patterns you now see? Or have you narrowed to one amazing, beautiful thing?

Maybe you don't see any of that. Maybe you're looking at your list and thinking, "There's no way I could ever do any of this stuff on my list and turn it into a career."

I took my client Angela through these exercises and, at the end of the day, there were only two things on her list that got Yesssssses:

- Reading self-help books.
- Talking about life to my best friend.

Angela looked at her list and she told me she thought this was all stupid and she should just figure out how to deal with her Soul-sucking job. "If I work fewer hours," she argued, "then I can pick up some projects or hobbies I like."

"That's an option," I told her, "but it's also a way of avoiding claiming the joy of actually doing what you love."

She didn't see how reading self-help books and talking to her friends could ever be a career. And, yet, today she runs a seven-figure publishing business and spends her days talking to authors about their self-help books. In fact, she helped me write this one!

Even the most absurd things on your list can turn into a lucrative career! You get there by staying open and being creative.

* * *

Anything you love can turn into a career. The woman who walks my dog once a week went from being married with a corporate job to being divorced and owning her own acreage, complete with dog park, dog grooming station, and a thriving pet-walking/pet-sitting business.

A gentleman I saw on TV did something similar. He went from being a lawyer to owning a business where he takes very energetic dogs on long nature hikes every day, combining his desires to avoid people, hang out with dogs, and hike in the mountains every day.

If the job you want doesn't exist, create it. Seriously.

Resistance – or push-back – might show up for you here. Something might whisper – or shout – in your ear that you aren't worthy, aren't trained enough, or couldn't possibly do that. Ignore that resistance and that voice, because it's not your Soul and it doesn't really know what it's talking about (we'll talk more about this in Chapter 9). For now, just tell that voice to shove it and continue along as if you have no obstacles in the world.

Own your Yesssss! job direction. Even if it scares the bejeebus out of you. *Especially* if it scares the bejeebus out of you. Remembering your body reading from the Body Guide exercise, how does this sit for you, now that you've done the job list and review exercise? Are you scared because a job that jumped out at you seems wrong for you? Or is it a scared-excited feeling that means you're heading toward something good?

Trust Yourself

We've covered a lot of ground. We have looked at things from all angles and from a lot of places in time during your life. We have gathered puzzle pieces and put together a puzzle.

That solution that you have right now? It might change for you. Probably not right away, but it might become something different when you become someone different. You can let this new version of you go when the time is right, and we've talked about how to do that.

The most important part of this whole puzzle isn't that you know what you want to do for a career now; it's that you've connected to your inner guides for solutions instead of looking outside for the answer. You now have tools that can help you in a number of amazing ways to find solutions to all kinds to the roadblocks and setbacks that life can throw your way.

You have connected to a part of yourself that you may not have realized was there. You have connected to parts of you that have been buried and lost. And that's the real amazing work that's been done. Because connecting to yourself to find the answers is the only way to bring lasting joy into your life and your work. The work itself isn't going to make you happy – not really. It's you being unapologetically yourself that brings that joy, satisfaction, and freedom in life.

The important lesson here? It's to trust yourself and shine.

* * *

What if you've done all the exercises and still aren't sure? That's okay! You get to try things out. Pretty much everything in life – with the exception of maybe your children – can be tested out and changed. Your marriage… well, let's say that you liked your partner at first but over time they became a jerk; you can divorce that person. Not liking your home? Move. Don't like your extended family? You don't owe them anything, and you can stop going to Thanksgiving (really!). Tried out a career you picked out by doing the exercises in this book, but ended up not liking it? No problem. You can learn the lessons from having done it and then go pick something else.

So many things in life that feel really permanent aren't. You can change your partner, your underwear, how you dress, the languages you speak, how you feel, the country you live in, your drink of choice, your vacation spot, what you do for

Christmas, who you see at Christmas, the car you drive, the amount of money in your bank account. Everything.

(But you can't change your kids. You're stuck with those adorable suckers forever.)

You can also try things out before you more fully commit to them. Do you want to become a doctor or nurse? Go volunteer at a hospital. Talk to doctors and nurses. Research – look things up. Interview – talk to people who do what you want to do. See if you can get hired at the entry level. Take a class. Take a free class from one of the top universities.

Get creative. Buy the supplies to create what you want to create. Do the thing you want to do. Be the thing you want to do. Live it. Breathe it. Test it out.

And if doesn't work out for you, move on to the next thing. There's always something else that can use your gifts, allow you to be of service, and make your Soul-self happy. You're never limited to just one career, with no other options. Be like a college co-ed on spring break for the first time: experiment. A lot.

Most importantly, remember to do all of this from a place of Soul. That's the place that gives you the answers. Don't listen to your Uncle Dan tell you that no one ever makes money doing what you want to. Uncle Dan doesn't have your incredible sass and moxie. Your mom doesn't have your gifts. You sister has no idea what it's like to be you. You partner isn't the one living your life (it might seem like it, since they, you know, live with you and all, but it's your life). *You*, and only you, have the inner answers you need.

* * *

Give yourself permission to fail at doing this book. Give yourself permission to have to repeat some of the exercises and the process. Give yourself time to really connect to your Soul. Figure out different ways than I have put in this book to deeply connect to your body and Soul. Give it time. Do it all again. Throw the book in frustration and then come back to it in a week or so. *Feel how you feel.* Let things unfold the way they're unfolding. There is no magic timeline for it all to start making sense. It will happen in its own sweet time, and that may be on a timeline that's much different than what you want it to be. Let it.

Failing isn't ever the problem. Not trying is. The more you allow yourself to give up when you want to give up, feel how you feel, and allow things to be what they are, the faster it will all come together. I know, it doesn't make any sense. But it's true.

I explained that theory to my friend Jasmine at a picnic last summer. A few weeks later, I saw her at school pick-up and she stopped me and said, "You know how you were telling me to try something that comes from a place of Soul?"

I nodded.

"How do I *do* that? I heard what you said, but I just can't pick anything. Would you work with me and help me figure out how to get started?"

Jasmine and I started working together and within a few weeks she had tried ten different things. Though none of them were quite right for her, just tuning in to and feeling what was wrong with each one was huge for her, because it gave her great information, straight from her Soul. Jasmine had been avoiding feeling anything for so long, she'd needed help to reconnect with her Soul. That's not failing, that's a huge success.

Just to be able to see and to start is 90 percent of the battle.

So, I'm curious... whatcha wanna when you grow up?

Whatever it is, sing it loud, sista!

CHAPTER 8

Pull It Off

"It always seems impossible until its done."
–Nelson Mandela

*"Nothing is impossible, the word itself says
'I'm possible!"*
–Audrey Hepburn

*"Whatever you're meant to do, do it now. The
conditions are always impossible."*
–Doris Lessing

To pull this off, you need to be ruthlessly intentional with your time. You need to know how you spend your time, what you can get rid of, when to hire support, how to tackle projects (like changing careers), and know why you're doing this crazy thing.

Time Currency

Time is a form of currency. We all have the same amount each day. We're all gifted with 86, 400 seconds, with 1440 minutes, with 24 hours in every day. How we choose to spend that time matters. It's everything.

There's a tendency to believe that there isn't enough time to do it all, but I'm going to tell you a secret: There is exactly the right amount of time each day to do everything that is important.

In fact, if you believe and constantly tell yourself that you don't have time, you make it true. If you tell yourself that you have exactly enough time to accomplish everything important, that becomes true instead. Try it!

Once you cut through the noise of what isn't really important to you and cut it out of your life, you're left with nothing but time for the things and people that are important to you.

Once you decide to unsubscribe from the drama, the excessive worry, and the things you really don't enjoy doing, you get to add in more of the things that are good for your Soul, add more love into your life, and generally make yourself feel the way you want to feel.

Your Time

So, what are you doing with your time? No, really, exactly how are you spending your time?

This is a pretty good example of how I spend my mornings:

- 5:30 – Wake up. Work-out (it's important for my mental health, so I do it first)
- 6:30 – Shower
- 7:00 – Get the kids up. Brush teeth. Tame hair. Get the kids water. Change a diaper. Stare bleary eyed at the fridge or counter for what to fix the kids to eat. Start breakfast
- 7:30 – Serve breakfast.
- 7:37 –Grab everything I forgot when I set out breakfast.
- 7:50 – Done with breakfast, tidy things up, get snack ready for school.
- 8:00 – Get the kids dressed.
- 8:10 – Leave to walk to school.
- 8:25 – Drop off five-year-old.
- 8:35 – Walk back home.
- 9:00 – Get the rest of my day started: go to the grocery store, do other errands, go to appointments. On some days, start work.

You can see that, in my world, with two handsome boys to wrangle, it takes almost four hours before I can start my work or accomplish anything on my non-kids to-do list.

Dinner, baths, and bedtime take another two to three hours of my day. Lunch and a quick catnap take another hour or more, depending whether I have my kids solo or if my husband is home.

Just getting to work time takes up half of my day. Gone. And I haven't yet gotten to errands, appointments, chores, school pickup, work, lunch, emails, clients, caring for my kids, entertaining my kids, walking the dog, Soul care, or socializing.

If I'm not ruthlessly intentional with my time, I can spend the entire day doing things in my home or with my kids that aren't important, don't need to be done, and haven't gotten me any closer to me dreams. Days turn into weeks, weeks into months, and eventually into years.

Instead, my time is spent exactly how I want it to be spent, on my four main priorities:

- My business.
- My two tiny humans.
- My husband.
- Being the best Domestic Goddess I want to be. (I totally hire out the rest, which we'll talk about soon)

Extra time needs are planned in advance or added in only *if* I want them to be. I use my Body Guide to figure that out.

Because I do have depression as a travelling companion through life, some days I can go like gangbusters and accomplish many, many, many things, but other days, when my depression flares, I can only do one small, tiny thing that moves me closer to my goals.

Sometimes that one small thing is clearing my schedule so I can rest for a day – because it's not all about accomplishing things as fast and as furiously as possible. It's about moving toward your goals and dreams of a wonderful career at a pace that you're excited about and able to maintain. Sometimes pushing, sometimes pulling back for a bit to allow life to be what it is. But always moving forward.

It all adds up in the end.

* * *

I learned some time ago that I needed to prioritize my time if I was ever going to get closer to doing work that lit me up. To do that, I had to see where I was spending my time each day and look at what could ultimately be left off my to-do list each day/week.

Now it's your turn. Grab your trusty journal or a piece of paper and a pen. Set the timer for 15-25 minutes. Let's look at your current life and how you spend your time.

- Starting Monday morning when you wake-up, what do you do? Itemize your day in as much detail as possible. How long does it take for you to wake up, brush your teeth, get dressed, have breakfast, clean up, feed your kid(s) get them ready, etc.?
- What do you do next? And then after that? Keep going until you reach bedtime. Do this for three or

so days, until you get a really good picture of how you're spending your time each day.

- Then, get into Body Guide mode and look at all those items while getting a read on how you *actually* feel about each of them. I bet you'll be surprised.
- Now divide the daily tasks into four categories: Awesome, Pretty Good, Meh, and Nope!

The Awesome zone is your area of genius. It's all the things that you do that, when you do them, you end up in a place of flow. It's all of the things you *love* to do and don't want to give up. Things that, if you were to spend all of your time doing them, you would be so happy you would cry. My Awesome zone list has things on it like coaching, writing, baking, going for hikes in nature with my family, brainstorming, and business planning.

The Pretty Good zone is for all of the things that you're really good at and you enjoy, but you don't love them like the Awesome flow zone things. You would be pretty satisfied if the things on this list made up your entire day. In my Pretty Good zone, I have doing budgets, creating content, marketing, and doing my taxes (really, I'm a big nerd).

The Meh zone is where you put all the things that, technically, you *can* do but you really don't like to do. For me, things like meal planning or dishes or shopping go here.

The Nope! zone is for all the of dreaded, hated tasks. Put things in this zone if you would celebrate never having to do it again. My Nope! zone includes shopping for boring things, cleaning the bathroom, brushing or bathing my dogs, deep cleaning my house, and tracking expenses.

The goal is to get your life so cleared out that all the things on the Meh and Nope! zones are done by other people and you get to spend all of your time doing the Awesome and Pretty Good zone things all the time, because you've delegated or hired out the Meh and Nope! stuff.

Does it sound too good to be true that you could live your life only doing the things in the first two categories? Maybe a bit like someone would have to pinch you to make sure you're not dreaming? Like you're getting away with something sinfully delightful? Good! It should feel exhilarating to think about it. Attach to this feeling, because you can use it to keep yourself going when the going gets tough.

* * *

When I offered this exercise at a mini-retreat that I ran, a lot of the moms there were a shocked at how little time they really had left over at the end of the day, once they looked at how long it actually took to make meals, clean up the meals, go to work, and all the other things that creep into the days. But they were also surprised at how many things popped into their days that they didn't want there. Like guilt, worry, stress, drama, and overwhelm.

One mom talked about her guilt and reluctance to get down on the floor to play Lego with her kid when he asked. She would often say no because she loathes playing with Lego, and then would spend so much time feeling guilty over saying no that she would eventually end up playing anyway. She thought that, to be a good mom, she always had to do the things her kid wanted to do with her.

That's simply not true! Your kids want and need the best version of you that you can possibly deliver, and if that means that you say no to Lego playtime (which you loathe) and yes to the crazy 4 p.m. dance party (that you love) that your kids ask you for, then you get to show them how to put up their own beautiful boundaries and say no to things that don't light them up. Your kid can play Lego on their own (independent play is good) or with a friend, and you get to clear some energetic space from guilt and unhappiness from your day and spend that time doing something else. Something Awesome or Pretty Good.

Or, if Lego is *the* thing that your kid adores and saying no feels wrong to you, check in with your body and see how long you can play Lego before wanting to scream. It might be as little as five minutes. Set a timer for whatever feels best in your body and let your child know that when it goes off, you will be done playing until another day. Everyone wins.

By clearing anything that's on the negative Body Guide scale from your life, you end up with all kinds of energy and time to be doing things you really want to be doing – like gearing up for that new career or business. As an added bonus, your days start to feel more like how you really want them to feel – more fun and adventurous. Or calm and peaceful. Or whatever your Soul is yearning for.

Support

You can't buy more minutes in the day, but you can pay to have things taken off your plate, leaving you with more time to spend elsewhere. The time you spend doing only the things you care about with the people you love the most will ultimately add up to one amazing life that's the cat's meow.

So, how do you clear things off your plate?

You support yourself. Be kind to yourself. You know that your peace of mind and sanity are worth more than anything.

Write up your to-do list for the next day the night before. Write down everything that you have to do. Now cross off about 50 to 75 percent of the list. Seriously.

What's left is what you will really have time and energy for and can realistically accomplish. Leaving everything on your list is setting yourself up to fail by heaping on enough tasks that there's no way even Superwoman could accomplish them all in a day.

And then gift yourself some extra peace and sanity by learning to write down only the things that *need* to be done and can be realistically done in one day. Nothing more.

Now, take a look at some long-standing items on your to-do list that make you feel anxious and guilty because you haven't done them. Take a deep breath and let them go. If you haven't done them in a long time and they're still lingering on there, release them from your list of obligation and know that if they're important or need to be done later, they'll make it back on your list when you're better able to get them done.

As for the rest of it, prioritize your list for each day by doing the one thing you dislike the most first. By putting that at the front of your list you'll make sure it gets done and it will set you up for the rest of the day.

Add in time for Soul-Care. Give yourself some time to just breathe each day. Be kind to you, even if that's only five minutes spent caring for yourself in an intentional and kind way.

* * *

I know. Now you're wondering about the things that you crossed off your list but that still need to be done. Like cooking or laundry or grocery shopping. You have options! The point of this whole thing is to help you figure out creative solutions that you may not have thought of yet.

If there's something you hate, just stop doing it! Hate dusting? Stop doing it. Don't like cleaning up your kids toys and they're old enough to help? Stop doing it. Don't like paying your bills every week? Put them all on auto-payment and deal with it once a month. Don't like housecleaning in general? Hire a cleaner. Pay someone to do your laundry or pick up your dry cleaning.

No extra room in the budget for that? Then do a trade with someone. Get your neighbor to pick up groceries for you while you pick up your and their kids. Find someone who wants monthly massages in exchange for personal training or pedicures. Bake someone's birthday cake in exchange for some freezer meals. Trade childcare with your bestie so you can get stuff done and take time for yourself. *Get creative.*

Use those gifts of yours to take stuff you don't want to do off your plate. Practice those receiving and giving skills!

Can't trade it or pay someone to do it for you? Then find a way to make it more pleasant. Maybe write in your journal and ask your Soul-self what it would take for you to spend an hour or two each month happily paying some bills instead of dreading it each month. The time you spend worrying and stressing about something each day/week/month is valuable time you could be spending doing more pleasant things.

Maybe your always-entertaining Soul-self tells you that, for the pleasure of performing this unpleasant task, you're going to need to allot an equal amount of time for watching Prancersise videos and cat videos on YouTube while eating fancy chocolates and drinking champagne. *Do that.* Plan to do the balancing-out fun time after the yucky task. You'll find that paying those bills probably won't be so bad with such an amazing and hilarious reward at the end.

Your Rhythms

There will be times when you find yourself unable to do as much as normal. You will most likely feel frustrated by this and want to fight it. Don't.

We all have rhythms. Much like Momma Nature has seasons, we all have times when we're productive and able to accomplish *all* the things and times when we want to hibernate and eat all the chocolate in bed.

In the bigger picture view, you might find that you're more active and alert during spring and summer and more sedentary and not able to do as much in the fall or winter. Or you might feel a lull right as the seasons change, but then you adjust and feel good. *Notice.* How is your energy, generally, during each season?

Each month you might find that there are a few days, or even a couple of weeks, when you don't have the same amount of energy as you do during the rest of the month. That may be tied to your period; it might be tied to something else. *Notice.*

Each week, you may find that there are one or two days when you are so very lazy and one or two days when your energy overflows and you can do more. *Notice.*

Each day, there will be natural highs and lows in your moods and energy. Maybe you feel tired and sluggish until noon and then wake right up until midnight. Maybe you need an afternoon nap each day at 2 p.m. *Notice.*

As you spend some time to really notice your rhythms, notice your more energetic times of the day and schedule in the harder, more tiring tasks for then.

You won't be doing yourself any favours if you're constantly trying to fit in a workout or coursework right when your body is screaming for rest and a nap. Learn to work *with* your rhythms. It will save you a ton of stress.

If you are in a low-energy time and have to accomplish things anyway, be as kind to yourself as possible. Allow more time, schedule a nap for immediately afterward, plan some awesome Soul-Care, and, most importantly, don't beat yourself up. Honour your body and its rhythms and you'll find yourself much more able to accomplish your goals. It sounds counter-intuitive, but it's true!

* * *

A client of mine, Sherry, was beating herself up a lot because it seemed like she gained a lot of traction in her business sometimes but then it would fall apart and she would end up with low energy, due to exhaustion, depression, and headaches. She would give up and not do anything at all during those times, and it felt like she always had to begin again each time it passed.

We talked about her rhythms and I gave her the task of tracking the times of low energy and depression. It turned out that, despite the hysterectomy she had gotten years before, and in spite of never having a period anymore, her body still worked on those rhythms of her cycle. Her times of depression and anxiety were worse for about a week or two every month to six weeks, and she felt unable to do much in the way of work during those times.

When Sherry understood more about what was happening for her, she was able to schedule things in a way that allowed for less to be done during those physical downtimes. Best of all, once she understood what was happening, she stopped beating herself and, instead, embraced those physical cycles as a necessary times to rest more and enjoy some downtime. She even started to look forward to the break in her life that those times allowed her.

Big, Beautiful Boundaries

Boundaries are how you keep things manageable in your life. You, and you alone, are in charge of your life. You get to decide all the things that you will and will not allow to come into it.

How do you shut out the noise and find the time and energy for yourself and your new career plans? By setting big, beautiful boundaries.

First, let's take a look at what happens when boundaries aren't so good.

Weak Boundaries

If you have extra time, as a busy mom, it will fill up. Everything in your life demands your attention: little ones who need you, the pile of dishes in the sink, your partner who you haven't look properly at in ages, your dog to walk and brush, the workout you need to do, the pile of bills to pay, the walls to remove sticky finger marks from, the play date to attend, the cold coffee to reheat, the nap you need to take, the appointments to book, the friends to catch up with, books to read, shows to watch, groceries to buy, laundry to fold, the thousand online distractions, and the thousand parts of the house you haven't had time to clean in ages. Whew! There's always something and someone else to put first, demanding more from you.

Now, imagine that you are standing out in the rain. The rain represents all the things that life asks you to do. Each drop is an item on your to-do list – someone who needs something from you, things you want to do.

When you have weak boundaries, it's like you're standing out in that rain wearing a sweater with only a folded up newspaper to keep you dry. Someone, at some point, told you that it was normal – desirable, even – to stand out there in the rain all the time and get soaking wet. At first, your sweater keeps the rain off of you and you are warm and dry for a little while; everything is just fine. But, eventually, the more it rains, the more your sweater and that newspaper end up soaked through. All the things vying for your attention are winning, and you end up wet, cold, frustrated, perhaps even a little angry that the rain *just won't stop*! Resentment pops in. If you're not careful, it will set up shop and stay.

Sure, sometimes the rain slows down and the sweater dries out and it's all good. But then it begins to rain again. Each time that happens, you're less and less okay with getting soaked all over again and being wet most of the time, but you can't get yourself out the rain. You're not sure how to go about doing that.

This is when you develop Superwomanitis. This happens when you believe that you have to stay out in the rain wearing that sweater – cold, wet, angry, and unhappy – and that you have to catch each rain drop as it falls. Or else.

You feel pressure, expectation, and a desire to be competent. You never want to let anyone down. Never want to say no. Think that you're the only one who can do it right.

You can't bring yourself to get out of the rain.

This thinking is dangerous. Why? Because, if left untreated, it creates overwhelm, frustration, exhaustion, burnout, and

– at its worst – crippling self-doubt and a tendency to resent your life.

Healthy, Strong Boundaries

Healthy, flexible boundaries come from deciding that you're going to buy yourself a warm coat and an umbrella to keep the rain off of you. You decide how much rain you want and how much you can deal with easily. When you're tired of the rain, you go inside the house! You do some Soul-Care. You decide that you will not be Superwoman. You will not expect yourself to do it all. You will learn where your boundaries are, honour them, and maintain them.

This is what having healthy boundaries looks like:

- Say no. A lot.
- Only say yes when your Body Guide reading is high. In other words, if it's not an immediate, excited Yessss, it's a no.
- Delegate.
- Ask for help – free or paid or in trade.
- Know when you need time to rest and do so.
- Be okay with disappointing people. Don't expect people to always say yes to you.
- Honour your rhythms, your Body Guide, and your energy levels.
- Regularly clean out anything that isn't serving you anymore, whether it's a thing, a thought, a Meh, or a Nope!

- Know that getting something done is better than getting it perfect.
- Know that your worth in life has nothing to do with how many things you strike off your to-do list each day.
- Know that your needs, wants, and desires are as important as everyone else's – including your partner's and children's.
- Be incredibly kind to yourself and others, but also don't others walk all over you.
- Plan your life with your goals in mind and say no to things that don't get you closer to reaching them or that don't make you feel the way you want to feel.
- Connect to your Soul and your heart for your answers – nowhere else.

As a start to putting up your big, beautiful boundaries, you need to learn when they are being crossed. This takes practice. The clues for this are feelings of anger and frustration. When you feel angry over something – and since you are now feeling your feelings, you will feel anger at times – you can question it and find out where a boundary has been crossed.

Let's say that you've had a tough day at home with a sick kid. You were up most of the night, have been vomited on twice, and haven't had a chance to shower. All you want is one long, hot, delicious shower; a big sandwich; and a 30-minute nap. You eagerly wait for your partner to get home so you can get those things you need.

He walks in the door and, without more than a hello, jumps in the shower ahead of you.

You're livid. He knows that you've had a tough day – you've been texting all day to give him updates – so why should he get to go shower first, when you've been vomited on all day?!

He comes out and you unleash on him. He answers that he wanted the shower out of the way so he could take over as fast as possible for you, but you don't hear him because you're too angry. It causes a big fight.

Communication breakdown aside, what you're really angry about isn't that he had a shower; it's that your tough day wasn't acknowledged. Your needs weren't being met *in the way* you needed them to be. You needed support, you needed communication. You needed a hug!

The question to ask yourself as soon as you feel angry, frustrated or anything in between, is: "Where have my boundaries been crossed? What am I really angry about?"

When you know the reason your boundaries have been crossed, you can do something to make sure it doesn't happen again. You can acknowledge what you need so that, next time, you'll be better able to articulate it and get your needs met. In this case, a quick text before your husband got home – to say that you got dibs on the shower the second he gets in the door, and right after he gives you a hug – could have helped with holding the boundary.

* * *

You really do have the time and energy to do the things that are important to you. If you get rid of the rest. When you're committed to how you want to feel in your life and you do the things you need to do in order to feel that way – you can be guilt-free! You know your worth and what makes you happy and you only let in the things that get you there.

I want you to thrive. I want us all to thrive. In order to thrive we need to learn our limits, put up strong but flexible boundaries, and be of service where and when we can... but no more than that.

* * *

My client, Maisie, first came to me with the goal of being able to do more in her business than she was doing at that time. She had big goals to travel – with and without her family – and to pay for it with the money her business would make.

When I asked her what was stopping her, she gave a long list: She didn't have a designated office; she couldn't work with all the clutter in her house; no one in her family was helping her to clean; her husband worked from home and disturbed her. All of those things were valid reasons why she couldn't do her work and build her business. It *is* hard to do work when your family won't leave you alone. It *is* hard to accomplish a lot when you're the only one cleaning up. It *is* hard to build a business when you're trying to do it all, be it all, and have it all.

We worked on helping her put up some flexible boundaries that worked for her and her family. She started to see that a lot of what was stopping her were things *she* was allowing to stop her. There was no reason why Maisie's twelve-year-old and six-year-old couldn't help out around the house or learn to leave Mom alone for periods of time while she worked. There was no reason why Maisie needed to be the one to clean the house, ignoring her own work and goals, while her husband worked.

By the end of our work together, Maisie had asked her kids to help more, and they were. She understood the value of putting her needs on the same level as her family's needs.

* * *

What does this have to do with starting a new career or business? You're not going to be able to find the time and energy for it if you're worried about doing and being everything for everyone else. Much like getting to choose how you feel in your life, you get to *choose* where your time and energy goes and what's important to you to spend them on.

Mindful, Tiny Steps

When looking at the size of your goal for your new career or business, it may look and feel *huge*. Possibly even impossible.

Stop thinking of it like that, immediately! From now on, since you know how you want to feel in your life and how you want to feel once you've gotten from here to there, only think of the end result in terms of *how you're going to feel.*

Stop your brain from imagining every little, medium, and big step that's between now and then, and, instead, start to think about what it's going to *feel* like to get there.

Write those feelings down on the top of a page in your journal. Make them pretty, if you wish to. They really are the focus for you and they're what you're going to hold on to when the going gets tough – and it will, just so you know, but we'll talk about that more in Chapter 9.

Now break down the steps you'll need to take between now and when you have those feelings because you've reached your goal.

As you break down the steps, you'll most likely find that some of the steps will fill you with panic or dread. That means that the step is too big. Break those steps down even further into smaller steps.

Here's a way to get a sense of what pace to aim for. Imagine a proud, majestic, dazzling unicorn. Now imagine that this unicorn is the size of a mouse and it doesn't like to run. Instead, she likes to walk. Slowly. Like a sloth. With tiny steps. That pace is how your steps should feel when they're broken down: slow and steady steps that will add up to meeting your goal of a new career or business without causing you to want to flee to another country to recover your sanity.

Nice and easy. Slow and steady.

Go only as fast, and take on only as much, as your Body Guide tells you feels good. Every step you take, big or small, is going to get you there. Some days you'll have energy and time to do a lot and other days you'll barely get anything done. But you will still get there.

This is not about just looking at your progress on any individual day, but instead about how all those days and steps add up.

Planning

Look at that page on which you wrote your desired feelings – the feelings you want to have when you've reached your goal. Your next step is to write out your plan.

You can tape large sheets of paper to a wall and gather some pretty pens or markers. Write your end goal at the bottom of the last sheet. At the top of the first sheet, write where you are now. The space in between is where you'll fill in – and likely need to break things down further – in order to fill in the steps you'll need to do between now and your goal.

Are you planning on going back to school to learn something new? Your last step will be something like "write exams" or "hand in my last paper." If those feel too big and not at all like a slothy unicorn step, break them down even more. Yes, you can break steps down to "Put pants on," "Eat breakfast," "Get in car," "Drive to school," "Park car," and so on. Seriously, you can, and maybe you should, get that detailed. Go as detailed as you need to in order to get that sloth-unicorn pace feeling.

Research the parts of the journey you're not sure of. Will you need certification or need to join an association in order to do your new career?

Figure out all the steps and then break them down onto a timeline by putting dates at the milestones along the way. Yes, this may change, but that's okay.

By the time you've got it all up on those sheets of paper, you'll have a pretty solid idea of what you need to do to accomplish the next steps – all the way to your goal.

Commitment!

Remember that boyfriend you had who didn't want to call himself your boyfriend even though you hung out with each other exclusively and did all the things couples do all the time? Remember the level of frustration you felt because he. Just. Wouldn't. Commit?

Don't be that kind of boyfriend to yourself. Commit to doing this Soul-Care process for yourself. Commit so hard that there's no doubt that this career or business is the newest love of your life. Commit so much that your partner starts to get a little jealous. Fall in love with the possibilities that this career/business will bring you. Fall in love with how you're going to feel when you've met your goal, and how you feel now, as you start this amazing new adventure in your life. Love it hard, with all you've got.

There's a magic thing that happens when you commit to something in a really *big* way. All kinds of thing open up. Wonderful opportunities, delicious synchronicities, and fun adventures come into view. When you commit and go all-in on something that you want with all your heart, the Universe or God or whatever you want to call it, answers with powerfully good things. There's magic in the commitment.

Go all in on *you*, darling! Strive for what you want, but also remember to relax and have an amazing time as you go. After all it's really about the journey, not the destination.

"Life is a dance between making it happen and letting it happen."
– Arianna Huffington

CHAPTER 9

The Obstacles

*"I'm not telling you it's going to be easy - I'm
telling you it's going to be worth it."*
–Art Williams

*"It does not matter how slowly you go as long
as you don't stop."*
–Confucius

There are two things and two things only that will
get in your way of making this happen: your own
thoughts and your own resistance.

Your Thoughts

Leanna kept buying toys for her son and wanted me to
coach her about how to stop so that she could save some

129

money. After a coaching session or two, she discovered that, underneath it all, she was feeling guilty about her son being an only child, so she bought him toys to help alleviate her guilt.

She believed that she needed to give her son more than she already was.

When she questioned those thoughts, she realized that she was actually pretty happy with having one kid, especially since her little boy has cerebral palsy, a disease that requires a lot of care. After realizing that she didn't have to believe or act on those "buy him toys now" thoughts, she was able to stop. She now buys him toys when she really wants to, not when she's being "told to" by her guilty thoughts as a way of avoiding an uncomfortable feeling.

* * *

Your mind and the thoughts you think are going to be your biggest obstacles.

If you think that you will never have time to pull this off – you'll be right, because you think it, and you'll create more ways to prove you're right.

If you think that your dreams don't matter and that you don't have anything to offer – you'll be right, and you'll create more ways to prove that you're right.

If you think that later is a better time for this to happen – you'll be right, and you'll create more ways to prove that you're right.

We all have thoughts and beliefs that run on repeat and keep us stuck. It's like your brain picks certain songs to play over and over again, for whatever reason, even to the point that you're so sick of it you could vomit. That song, in this analogy, represents one thought or belief that you might have, or a collection of thoughts which, all put together, make up a story you tell yourself.

Leanna believed that she needed to have more kids in order for her son to be okay. When she thought that, she immediately felt like she needed to buy something to make it up to him. She did that for *years*! Until we worked on challenging those thoughts, and then her pattern changed.

You can change any of your "stories," but only if you get so sick of that song that you decide to get brave and change it to a new one.

Changing Your Thoughts

How does one change a repeating, habitual thought, exactly? I'm glad you asked. My favourite way – and there are many – comes from Russ Harris' book *The Happiness Trap*.

Let's say you have this thing you want to do – like assembling some furniture. Furniture gets put together all the time. There is nothing overtly good or bad about assembling furniture. Objectively, you have a pile of pieces that need to go together and be held together with other smaller pieces. Kinda boring really.

So, here's the fact: This table needs to be assembled. It's a job like any other job.

What gets tricky is when I put a meaning on this that makes it good or bad.

Me, a decade ago, would have been slightly panicked and grumpy at having to assemble a table. I would have started to have thoughts like, "I am a terrible furniture-assembler. Why did I think I could do this? I'm probably going to screw it up. Or put a piece on backwards and then have to redo the whole thing. Everyone is going to laugh at this table. Why am I even bothering to try? I'll just hire someone to do it. That's easier. And then no one will mock it." I would feel like an awful, inept, failure who couldn't do anything right.

Because of a coffee table.

I put a lot of *meaning* behind not being able to do something well that needed to be done. I made my not being able to do it well mean that I couldn't do much of anything well, which wasn't true. I had and have many talents and gifts, but coffee table assembly wasn't one that I immediately knew how to do well.

In a similar way, Leanna made only having one kid a bad thing because she made it mean that her son's life was lacking. She dealt with it by buy things for her son, but they were really to make it better for her.

You might be thinking that there's no way you can pull off a career change. Or that life is too busy. Or that you're not talented enough. Or that your gifts aren't as good as everyone else's. Or that you're too scared to make changes. Or that your good-enough job is fine, even though it makes you miserable. Any thought or belief you have that causes you pain or causes you to spiral down into depression, sadness, frustration, or anger is fair game to apply this method to.

Get ready to challenge your thoughts in a couple of super-simple steps.

1. **Notice the thoughts/belief/story.** Notice where you get sick of your own behavior or where you tell yourself untrue or unkind things. Notice what you tell yourself when you start to go down into the shame/anger/frustration spiral. Use the casual observer stance and be the one who is watching your thoughts as they go by.

2. **Interrupt the story you're telling yourself by putting some words in front of it.** Russ Harris uses the phrase "I'm having the thought that..." to preface his thoughts, beliefs, and stories. "I'm having the thought that I am terrible at building furniture." "I'm having the thought that my son needs more toys to keep him busy." This interrupts the power and flow of your thoughts and lets you observe them. You, not your mind chatter, can see the thoughts without attaching to them. This helps with stopping the tailspin of feeling like a failure or unhappy or sad or incompetent.

3. **Notice what happens when you put words in front of your thought.** Do the emotions that come up with the thought/belief/story ease off? Do you feel relief – even a little?

4. **Check to see if it's a whole story you're telling yourself.** Is this a whole story you're telling yourself vs. a single thought? Is it part of something bigger?

For example, my "I'm bad at assembling furniture" thought was part of a bigger story I told myself about how no one liked me. If I put together furniture badly, then it would one more reason why people would think I was unlikable.

5. **Name the story.** I would call it my Furniture Story when I thought the thoughts that led me down the rabbit hole to sadness and woe. That helped me interrupt those thoughts. "Oh, hello there. I recognize this thought. It's part of my Furniture Story, and I know that going there means I'll feel crappy, so let's not do this. I'll think about my kids instead.," and my crazy, Furniture Story-telling mind was more than happy to be given such a fun task (my mind *loves* thinking about my boys).

Unraveling Tangled, Messy Thoughts

Your mind will most likely rarely have a simple thought like the one in my furniture story. More often, you're going to have a wild, tangled mess of things all tied together that will feel impossible to unravel – like my client Maisie, who couldn't focus on one issue without jumping into how it affected everything else. To her, it was all just one ball of mess. Her work was tied to her home, which was tied to her marriage, which was tied to her belief that she shouldn't remarry because people in her family only married once and, besides, her kids were too important to her to introduce the mess of dating and potential attachment issues that would be involved.

It all *seemed* very tied together, but at the heart of it was her feeling of being trapped in a marriage to someone she'd chosen when on the rebound from her great love. Her Trapped Story, as she came to call it, echoed through everything else she experienced, and caused everything to grind to a halt – especially her business.

We used the thought work technique above and Maisie started to feel less trapped as she saw that the stories she was telling herself about her marriage were affecting everything else. She was able to find enough freedom enough from those thoughts to book a trip away. During that trip, she found enough release from her Trapped Story, and enough connection to her Soul, to figure out the next steps to take regarding her marriage and her business.

You can decide how you want to feel, decide which thoughts to believe, and do the work to untangle seemingly complicated things into simpler, more core thoughts and thus get yourself out of your own way and into the career and life you really want. It just takes a wee bit of courage and some willingness to try things a new way.

Resistance

> *"Most of us have two lives. The life we live, and the unlived life within us. Between the two stands Resistance."*
> **–Stephen Pressfield.**

You know that feeling of wanting to work out and actually making the time to do so and then sitting on your couch, unable to move? Or the feeling of knowing you have a deadline and yet do things like get on Facebook or watch one more episode of *Suits* instead? Or the feeling of knowing that you want to eat better to feel better but instead open that bag of chips? Or that other thing that gets in the way of you going out there and making a new career happen? Or the thing getting in the way of you starting that meditation, prayer, or yoga practice?

Meet resistance. Resistance, more than anything else, is the destroyer of dreams.

We all know what we want to be doing. We all know what would make us happier, healthier, and feel more loved, but how often do we jump right into doing it. Resistance is a vindictive harpy.

Resistance will show up every step of the way. Resistance is the cataclysm that shows up to knock us off our path. Resistance is the excuses we tell ourselves. Resistance is perfectionism. It's exhaustion. It's feeling like things need to be different before we can begin or finish anything that really matters to us.

Resistance is a liar.

It will tell you that watching Netflix is better than writing a book. It will tell you that one more glass of wine is a good idea. It will tell you that eating more is okay since it's Sunday. It's what tells you to sleep in instead of putting on your running shoes and going for a run. It's the thing that tells you that your deepest dreams are stupid, and that you're not able to accomplish anything.

Resistance tells you that it's someone else's battle to fight. That you can't make a difference; you're only one person. That everyone else is better suited to have their dreams come true. It's the part that agrees with you when you have the thought that you can't do things. When you think about giving up, Resistance will tell you that it's a good idea to do so – after all, you have so much on your plate right now. How much more can be expected of you?

You are not alone in your resistance. Everyone fights it. Everyone! We are all in this together.

The most important thing to know about resistance is that it exists. The second most important thing to know is that the bigger your calling toward something, the bigger the resistance you will feel.

Let that sink in for a moment. Whatever it is that you'd been dismissing or running away from but now that you're in talks with your Soul you can see more clearly and it seems big and scary but also exciting – *that* is the exact thing that you need to run toward and do.

What have you been resisting? What have you dismissed? What have you skipped doing in this book? Go back and do it now.

Beating Resistance

We all struggle with resistance and we all beat it in different ways. The best way, though, is to know that it exists, that's it's going to happen, and that once you've named it and committed to taking even one tiny step, and then some big steps, forward, it loses its power.

Taking action defeats resistance. It's the only thing that does.

Once you recognize resistance for what it is, feel the fear that often comes with it, and decide to do the work anyway, you've won. It's that simple. And that hard. Resistance is tricky and will show up in new and shiny ways once you've unmasked it. Look for it. Be on guard. Challenge it when you see it, by taking a step forward.

Create a game. Become a Resistance Hunting Superhero and make it your mission to find and fight the bad guy: Resisto. Keep the streets of your mind and life clean from the villains of Toxic Thoughts and Beliefs that work in cahoots with Resistance. The more you find them and eliminate them, the more you win at life.

How Resistance Might Show Up

Life, when you're all ready to make a big change, will want to really double-check and make sure that you're committed to this new adventure. It will really want to make sure that you're *sure* and that you won't quit when things get a bit tough. The way that this shows up is generally in the form of an Epic Cataclysm (aka resistance on steroids).

What is an Epic Cataclysm, you ask? Well, it's exactly what it sounds like. You'll be well on the path of your newest adventure and moving along nicely when – *Bam!* – you and your entire household will get sick with the worst flu imaginable. For a month straight. Or you'll have to move somewhere else. Or your car will implode and you'll need a new one. Or you'll get into a car accident. Or there will be an ant infestation. Or you'll throw your back out. Or sometimes it seems really positive at first, like a raise for your partner, or a promotion that means a move somewhere new. And then it all blows up into an Epic Cataclysm that means you stop going forward.

There will be *something* that comes along and tries to derail you. This something will take your time and focus away from your goal and make it seem like it wasn't really what you wanted anyway. You'll be really tempted to believe this something and want to give in and quit.

You'll begin to believe that it's not a great time right now to take even tiny steps forward with your plan. You'll question whether your dream is worth it. You might even tell yourself that dreams are stupid anyway, and that it's better to stay where you are. The things you already have will develop a lovely, warm glow to them and they will seem really comfortable and just fine. You'll feel and extra grateful for what you have. You will want to stay here for a while longer. It really isn't so bad here after all.

You can't control the unexpected things that come along. They're going to happen and your life is going to get disrupted, no matter how well you prepare. The trick isn't to try to prepare for everything – you can't – but instead to let that commitment you made with your Soul-self remain safe and secure in the background while you deal with the things that need to be dealt with.

You can be interrupted, derailed, hunched over in the worst of the Epic Cataclysms imaginable and still hold onto your dream. It doesn't really matter how much time passes between now and reaching your goal – the time passes anyway; you might as well be taking the little steps to be getting where you ultimately want to go.

Decide in advance how you're going to handle it when resistance or a Epic Cataclysm shows up. Decide in advance that you'll take action then anyway.

* * *

Take a moment right now and think back to where you were exactly one year ago. How much has changed, even though you may not have had a lot of control over a lot of circumstances in your life? I bet it's a lot. Now imagine if you had begun this adventure of a new career a year ago. Imagine where you'd be right now if you'd done even one or two things to get you closer. Now imagine yourself one year from now. Where do you want to be then?

Maybe you're thinking that, if life is going to throw things at you, there's no point in even starting. As someone who started writing this book a few months ago, let me tell you that there is a point to it. I almost quit writing at least four times, but each time I did I heard this gentle, little voice agree that it would be okay to quit, but that maybe, before I did, I could just finish this one more bit of the book before I did.

My Soul-self bargained with me and got me to agree to write one more chapter. Then one more. And then maybe

I'd be willing to edit it. And perhaps compile it into a manuscript to submit. Each time I felt like quitting, my Soul-self reminded me that it's not about reaching the big goal that's the objective; it's about doing one tiny thing to move forward, even if that seems like the most pointless thing ever.

That Soul commitment I had is the reason why you're reading this book.

Don't get overwhelmed by your big, final dream and goal. Focus on the one tiny step forward you can take from where you are right now, even if you're in the midst of a Epic Cataclysm. You can't control all the things that happen along the way, but you can control what you do about them.

Go back to the basics:

- Remember that beautiful Soul of yours. Get still. Listen.
- Check in to find out what your Body Guide is telling you is right for you.
- Feel your feelings; no bottling them up.
- Check in with the glorious ways you want to feel.
- Remind yourself why you wanted to do this in the first place.
- Remember all those times you did amazing things under duress and came out loving life and loving yourself more for getting through it all.

The Others

You have a lot of people in your life who love you. Those people are going to try and take you down. Really. Changing careers or becoming the New Shiny You may cause some people to be snarky, rude, or mean to you. They might tell you to not be so ambitious or to be more ambitious. They might call you names or try and take you down a peg. They might try and convince you to blow off your work. They may make rude comments, say mean things, pick fights, or ignore you.

The good news here is that none of this has anything to do with you and everything to do with them. You probably won't have as much time for some of the people in your life. You won't have as much patience for dumb drama. You will be busy working on your own stuff. That's a natural part of life when you have small kids and life goals. Your circle will get smaller. That's a good thing, ultimately. Quality over quantity will be your new battle cry.

You get to smile your gorgeous smile and continue on your way, letting the others do and feel as they wish to feel about it. Because your journey is not about them. It's about you. Don't take the others' antics personally.

* * *

In a session we had before she left on her solo vacation, Maisie said she was really worried about how her husband was going to be able to handle things while she was gone. She worried that he wouldn't do things right for the kids and that his anxieties and fears about her trip would make her enjoy her time away less if she had to check in all the time.

I asked her if she would rather cancel her trip and stay home so that she could do everything herself and make sure it was done right, or if she could go and, instead, know that the kids would, at the very least, be cared for, fed, and loved – even if the way that happened didn't look *exactly* like what she would have done.

She said she would rather go and let go of how it "should" be done, but that her husband's anxieties were still going to wreck things for her.

We talked about boundaries and how Maisie couldn't control her husband's reaction to her going. She could only control her reaction to him, and she could choose to let him have his anxieties without taking them on. She felt good about trying that, and off she went on her vacation.

When she got back, she told me that she hadn't let her husband's "stuff" get in the way of having a fabulous time. She'd known why she wanted to go, she'd known that she had to go for herself, and she'd gotten on that plane and flown off on an adventure. She got her trip, her husband got to experience life with the kids solo, and her kids got to see her doing things for herself that made her happy.

Ignore the naysayers and their noise. Do your thing *and love it while you do it*. Like the rebel warrior that you are, shut out the resistance when it shows up like this.

The Old You

The old you is going to wage a fierce war to get you back into your old habits, where it's safe and comfortable and warm... and stagnant, boring, and dull. It's going to want to pull you back to watching four episodes of *Scandal* on Netflix while sipping a beer and eating delicious things. Although new you won't quite have the same appeal, at first, because it's going to be super scary, the new you is the reason you're going through all of this in the first place.

A few weeks into my divorce, as I was living out of suitcases in a windowless, cold, dark basement room at my parents' house, where my brothers had their small TV for video games, all I could think about was going back to my old, comfy, king-sized, fluffy bed in my old, bright, and sunny bedroom, with all my things in drawers and closets and my giant soaker tub in the bathroom waiting to let me sink down into warm, soothing comfort. I wanted the familiarity so bad.

But that comfy, king-sized, fluffy bed and my bright, sunny room came with a price tag: a marriage that didn't work for me anymore.

So I did what any person moving back to their parents' home after owning their own home and being married would do: I cried. I mourned. I felt my feelings. And I put one foot in front of the other, day after day, until it got easier. I became a new person. Painfully and slowly, I became the person I needed to be to get here, exactly where I want to be.

Let yourself become the new you that you want to be, even if it's crazy uncomfortable. The rewards will be so worth it.

Overwhelm

You're gonna feel overwhelmed at times. Guaranteed. This is another sneaky way resistance shows up. You'll be merrily going along and following your plan when life will pile things on you again. You'll be feeling the way you want to feel, taking care of yourself, and making progress and – *Bam!* – something will happen. It's normal. It happens to us all.

What you can do is decide, in advance, how you're going to handle it when such things happen. What will you do when *this* pops up? How about *that*? When you take a look at the path ahead with a view toward looking for potholes, you can decide ahead of time how you might deal with it. Then maybe you won't be so surprised that it's happening and you can go ahead and do what you need to get through it.

You'll need some extra Soul Care to get through it. Ask yourself what you need in that moment and then go do that thing. Check with your Body Guide. Don't try to be Superwoman. Take the easy road and ask for help. Go through your schedule and your to-do lists and decide what can be eliminated.

Go back to Chapter 3 and Chapter 8 and use those tools – over and over again, if you have to.

* * *

Which brings me to my next amazing nugget of truth to tell you all about: You get to decide exactly how happy you want to be!

You know that self-sabotage thing that a lot of us do? It's that thing we do when life is going really well and then there's a voice in our head that says, "Whoa, nelly! That's about enough happiness right there, so now it's time to Mess. This. Up." Resistance at its finest, really. We break off the relationships, pick a fight, mess up at work, get really sick at a critical time, and generally do everything we can to get right back to the "safe" levels of happy we're more familiar with – the levels where things are pretty good, but there's enough messiness around to keep us from getting uppity.

A lot of this is done subconsciously. You probably don't even realize that you're doing this. Or if you do, you might not know why. It's because, at some point in your journey as a human, you arbitrarily decided what your top happiness level could and should be and set the bar there so when you start moving past it at any point, the freak outs and sabotage begin.

You might have no clue that this happens. Or you might know exactly what I'm talking about and can see it happening but don't know how to stop it.

It's ridiculous if you really think about it. To think that there's a finite amount of happiness you're allowed and that if you're too happy it could get used up and you'd be a miserable person and everyone would hate you and throw pies in your face. That too much good will can and will cause more bad things to happen.

Let's decide to stop this stuff, okay? – the sabotage and the being scared that happiness might run out. Instead, let's pause in the moments just before messing things up, or immediately after (this is going to take practice after all), and replace that "oh no, I always mess things up" beating one's self up thing we do with some self-love, kindness, and understanding toward ourselves. Let's love the people we used to be and the mistakes we used to make and decide right here and right now to *raise* that happiness level up! Go higher. Ask for more from life and from yourself. Decide on a new level of happiness.

Choose to *be* the person who is extra, super-duper happy, *do* the things to get you there, and *have* that really amazing life and career.

If *happiness* isn't your favourite word, replace it in the paragraphs above with anything you want to feel (because you get to decide that for yourself, too) – like *love* or *joy* or *play* or *spaciousness* or *freedom* or *peace* or *abundance*. It all works.

* * *

Resistance and obstacles have shown up for me in a lot of ways and in a lot of places I didn't expect. I am constantly on guard for the new ways they will show up for me. I buy courses, hire coaches to help me find my own resistance and obstacles, and hire people to support me in my quest to help mommas free their Souls and find the best, more meaningful work that uses their gifts.

I have seen the many ways resistance has shown up for my clients. It showed up for Beth by telling her that she couldn't possibly take a course to become an interior designer, because that might throw her back into feeling depressed and low, when the reality was that, as soon as she got rid of her good-enough job at a bank and got to work as a designer, she felt far fewer periods of depression and low moods and, instead, found ways to pace herself while doing work that lights her up.

Resistance showed up for Anna in the form of thoughts repeated over and over again that she didn't have the time and energy since she has small kids, even though it had been her dream for over a decade to open her own dream inn. Through our work together, she has begun to see that her current position as a manager in a large retail chain makes her feel bored, restless, and unhappy enough to not enjoy a lot of her time with her family, and that taking the steps to do what she loves instead would make her happier and more able to be present with her family.

Resistance showed up for Maisie in the form of thoughts that she couldn't work without a "proper" and "tidy" work space and that she couldn't afford to pay for people to help her keep up her home. She spent hours cleaning house – a never-ending job – instead of working on her business. After we worked together, she saw that by paying someone to help her out, she was really paying for more time and freedom to grow her business and make more money, thus giving her more freedom.

Resistance and obstacles show up for us all. *We get to choose how we handle them.* Let's all decide, right here, right now, to work on finding out where resistance exists for us and to kick it to the curb. Okay?

CHAPTER 10

Conclusion

"This is the real secret of life – to be completely engaged with what you are doing in the here and now. And instead of calling it work, realize it is play"
–Alan W. Watts

"Hide not your talents, they for use were made, What's a sundial in the shade?"
–Benjamin Franklin

Y ou did it! You made it to the end of the book, and I am so happy that you did. Congratulations on knowing what you want to do next

You have all the tools to figure it out and, really, the only tools you need are the ones about going go within yourself to find the answers instead of looking outside.

You've met that beautiful Soul of yours and learned to connect with its messages. You've learned about listening to your body's wisdom as a guide. You can hear the whispers – or shouts – from your body and your feelings and recognize when something that seems like a really good idea to others may in fact a terrible idea for you, or when something that other people don't understand why you want is exactly what you need to do. That knowledge right there, the ability to know and do things that are right for you, despite what others may say – that's pure gold.

Arguably, one of the hardest but most important parts of this process is accepting and feeling your own feelings. Sounds simple. Surprisingly crazy hard to do. But if you get this down, and I know you have before, and can and will continue to do so, then things will start to open right up for you more and more. There is no more needing to hide, because there is nothing scary to stop you.

And, last, but definitely not least, you decide how you want to feel in your life. You can tell if you're on the right track toward your goal by the way you feel. Definitely not every minute of every day, but overall, you can look back and see the patterns of how you felt. Maybe they lined up with the path you want to be one and maybe they didn't quite, but with the tools you have, you can ask your Soul for help to get you on your way.

You've glimpsed the person you want to be, accepted the person you are, and moved on from the person you were. You see yourself and are on the hot track to really getting to know those gifts of yours that make you amazing.

You know what you want. You know what you have to offer. And you know the stuff that's going to get in your way – yes, there will be some of that. Possibly even a lot of it. But that's okay, because the end result is what you're going for, and the best way out of the mess is to go through it. Keep going. Even a tiny step and then another will get you there.

You have looked a whole lot at what you don't want, what you do want, what you want to take a stand against, and who you can help with your gifts. You know, even more clearly now, how resistance shows up for you and how you get in your own way. But you're not going to let it stop you anymore. Because you're a rebel.

Trust yourself. There are no wrong answers when it comes to you. There are only *your* answers. Trust that you know exactly what you need to do, even if it's hard. This trust piece might be the hardest part of the puzzle for you. Know that you're only going to get as far as you trust yourself to get. The dividends that are paid when you really, deeply listen to your Soul-Self are worth more than any other investment you can make. Count on yourself. Invest in yourself.

My biggest wishes for you are that you really see yourself – the deep-down, Soulful you – and see how beautiful you truly are.

Take your knowledge of your Soul, your gifts, and invest in your desire to find or create work that will light you up so much that you glow like the blazing noon sun. Find or create work that uses the gifts and talents you have been given, serves people in ways that make a difference in this world, and allows you time and energy to not only navigate the career change, but also to simplify your life so you can do more of what you want and less of what you don't.

Channel your fierce momma-bear energy into discovering ways to get stuff done. Wake up excited to go to work instead of dreading the week ahead on Sunday night. Have the time and the energy and ability to really be present and enjoy your family – every chaotic, love-soaked moment. Have more peace of mind and clarity about how you want to spend your time.

Go through your days feeling amazed and in awe of how much you love your work, your life, and your family. Feel like you have to pinch yourself daily to make sure you're not dreaming.

You won't be. It will all be real.

ACKNOWLEDGEMENTS

There are so many to thank for helping me get this book written; it definitely took a village.

First and most importantly, I want to thank my boys. Chris, my wonderful husband, thank you for being so patient, understanding, loving, and so willing to pick up the slack while I sat typing away – this book really couldn't have happened without you. Your belief in me along the way has been unwavering and has inspired me to keep going on those days when I wanted to quit. My adorable boys – thank you for the sneaky but sweet visits to my desk while your dad's back was turned, and for your patience while I was so busy and preoccupied with this book. I love you more than you can ever know.

To the grandparents – my mom and dad, and Sandy – who ever so graciously and kindly agreed to the extra kid-sitting shifts while I wrote this book. Your love and support means the world to me and this book definitely wouldn't have happened without your help.

Angela – thank you for creating the space for this book to happen and for teaching me more in nine weeks than I'd learned in years before. So much gratitude and love to you and for the vision that you hold for all of your incubating authors as we go from an idea to a book that matters and makes a difference in this world. A round of thank-yous to all the people on your team who brought this book to life. And some extra big hugs to you, Grace – your editing magic turned this book into something even better than I could have imagined.

Beverly – for all of your wisdom and guidance and for creating the Soul's Calling program, thank you! Without it, this book would have been impossible. Emma, Nicole, Lisa, Mihn, Joyce – my Soul sisters – thank you for your weekly presence, even when I couldn't be there with you, for holding space for this book to be created, and for your enthusiasm; it all means more to me than you can know.

Dearest Mananda, remember that time you gifted me a book on writing because I'd mentioned I was destined to write a book? I so did it! Your support then and now is appreciated. Love you, lady!

Laura, Gemma, Stacy, and all the other mommas who inspired me along the way – I am grateful to you for sharing your stories with me.

And, lastly, for everyone else who has given their help, love, support, enthusiasm, interest, and well wishes – I want you to know that it has meant the world to me.

To the Morgan James Publishing team: Special thanks to David Hancock, CEO & Founder for believing in me and my message. To my Author Relations Manager, Gayle West, thanks for making the process seamless and easy. Many more thanks to everyone else, but especially Jim Howard, Bethany Marshall, and Nickcole Watkins.

Much love and gratitude to you all!

ABOUT THE AUTHOR

Kayla Berg is an author and a Career and Life Coach for Moms. After more than a decade as a corporate drone in Soul-crushing jobs, she gave it all up to follow her dreams She now has it as her mission to help moms who don't know what they want to do for work to find the right job or business for them and their families so they can earn money doing work they love.

She completed her life coach training with the Martha Beck Institute and is an endorsed Soul's Calling Coach. She lives with her family in Alberta, Canada where she splits her time between family, work, and tracking down missing socks.

Website: www.kaylaberg.com
Email: info@kaylaberg.com
Facebook: www.facebook.com/kaylabergcoach

THANK YOU

You've done it, you've finished the book! Congratulations on taking the first steps toward your shiny new career. As a special thank you, and to help you find some delicious and decadent time for yourself so you can have the energy for said shiny new career, I've put together a *free* Frazzled to Free Toolkit complete with audios, meditations, and worksheets of exercises from the book just for you!

All you have to do to access it is to visit www. FrazzledToFreeBook.com/soulcare, enter your email for the download, and, voila, you'll be sent the whole shebang.

Enjoy!

Morgan James
Speakers Group

We connect Morgan James published authors with live and online events and audiences whom will benefit from their expertise.

Morgan James makes all of our titles available
through the Library for All Charity Organization.

www.LibraryForAll.org

CPSIA information can be obtained
at www.ICGtesting.com
Printed in the USA
BVOW08s2307271217
503860BV00001B/10/P